Manu FEILDEL

Manu's FRENCH KITCHEN

Photography by Chris Chen

LANTERN

an imprint of

PENGUIN BOOKS

For my son Jonti —
everything I do is for you

CONTENTS

INTRODUCTION

Memories of my upbringing and my family always seem to centre around food. I was born and raised in the north of France, in Nantes, one of the largest cities in the country. Nantes is in Brittany, a gorgeous region with its own strong cultural and culinary identity. The area is renowned for beautiful countryside and also for its amazing coastline – my family lived about an hour and a half from the Atlantic and we used to spend our summers by the sea.

Food-wise, we enjoyed the best of both worlds. From the sea, we were blessed with wonderful blue lobster, mussels, langoustine (like scampi), spider crabs, monkfish and oysters called fines de claire, which are famous all over France. From the land there was always the most fantastic seasonal produce available no matter what time of the year – artichokes, reinette apples, chestnuts, cauliflower (a personal favourite), fat juicy strawberries and vraic potatoes, which are fertilised using seaweed. Not to mention the village markets. Wow, these were (and still are) simply amazing! Every day a market would pop up in a different town or village and we could buy charcuterie by the weight, local cheeses, cider, honey and other traditional and homemade foods, all super-fresh and of the best quality.

And then there was the bread! The delicious smell of freshly baked bread is one of my strongest food memories. During the week Mum would give my sister and me a coin each and we'd buy ourselves a big, fat, squishy *pain au chocolat* on the way to school and that was breakfast. But come the weekend, we'd go out with everyone else to buy fresh bread, croissants and brioche from the bakery, then take all those lovely carbs home and have an absolute feast. We could smell the bakery way before we could see it, and that warm, inviting aroma is, to me, the absolute essence of not just my childhood but of France itself.

Most people associate France with romance and perfume, haute cuisine or haute couture. But when I think of France, what springs instantly to my mind are all the excellent, but often simple, dishes and ingredients that people there have access to every day (and that I was lucky enough to be exposed to when I was a boy). My mum was such a talented cook and my recollections of her food, and time spent around the family dining table, are the reason for this book. It's a tribute to my mum.

Mum is from Anjou, a region that borders Brittany. Her dad was a chef and her grandfather a pastry chef, but even with all those professionals in the family it was actually her mum who taught her how to cook. Although she worked full time and pretty much brought my sister and me up on her own, Mum always had made-from-scratch meals on the table for us, seven days a week.

She shopped for the entire week on Friday and often, because she loved to entertain, she'd spend the entire weekend cooking so friends and family could come and share her wonderful feasts. It was nothing for her to feed twelve people for Sunday lunch or dinner.

We never ate frozen food (or any other kind of convenience food) at home and it saddens me that today, even in France, the supermarkets are full of 'ready meals' and other products that I detest. The quickest dishes Mum made for us were her composed salads in the summer and superb vegetable-based soups in the winter, and even then, these were thoughtfully put together and not full of leftovers or things out of tins. And Mum never really cooked us separate meals or special foods when we were little, either. We learned to eat what the adults ate from Day One and I honestly believe this is the best way to get children to try everything – including vegetables. It develops their palates. I get annoyed with 'kids' menus' in restaurants as they usually feature junk foods like nuggets – as if children aren't capable of enjoying real food! The only thing I really hated growing up was liver, and I'm sure that's because our babysitter used to serve it to us so well cooked that it was practically cardboard. Actually I don't mind liver now – I've trained myself to eat everything. I honestly believe that when people say they don't like a certain food it's to do with some bad memory or association and they can school themselves out of it. Even with offal . . .

Mum's food, which forms the basis of this book, is traditional and quite rustic but full of flavour. Everything she made us she cooked with love, and I most adored her winter dishes. These were things like cauliflower soup (see page 56), veal blanquette (see page 120) and tarte tatin (see page 168). I call this food with 'balls' because it had so much of that up-front 'yum factor' and it was very unpretentious. The most important thing was never how it looked, but how it tasted.

For my family, sitting around the table together and filling ourselves with delicious food was a way of life. As we got older, my sister and I would help Mum out with the cooking and setting the table. This taught me early the team aspects associated with catering, and it stood me in good stead later when I became a professional chef. It's great to get kids involved in food preparation at home as I think it really helps develop a respect for food and cooking, plus a love for family mealtimes.

I'd love to say, especially as I come from a family of chefs (even my dad was a chef), that I always wanted to cook, but actually my real ambition when I was young was to join the circus! If you've seen me in action on TV you'll probably realise I love to perform. At home I was always playing the fool and was something of the family (and school!) buffoon. One day when I was a teenager Mum noticed a van pull up in town with 'Circus School' written on the side and enrolled me to learn circus craft. My trainers were a Romany family and they were incredible. There were mum, dad and three young kids and between them they did everything from the trapeze, tightrope walking, acrobatics, clowning and animal taming, to sewing costumes. I studied with them for several years before deciding I should maybe do something a little more practical with my life – so it was then, at fifteen, that I went to work in my dad's restaurant kitchen in Saint-Nazaire on the Atlantic coast. As I left home to work, the first chapter of my life with food ended, and a whole new one began. And this, as they say, is a whole other story (and one I'm planning to tell another time). You'll have to wait!

When I cook now, whether at home, on the road or in the restaurant, what I strive for above everything is to produce food with flavour like Mum's food. I've tried hard to do Mum proud by weaving her special 'flavour factor' throughout the recipes in this book, most of which are from her repertoire. The remainder are the classic French bistro dishes that make the crossover into the home. It's all relatively simple fare and not technically difficult to prepare. Some of the dishes will no doubt be familiar already – I'm not attempting to reinvent any wheels here! Every recipe is included because it's for a dish that makes me happy when I cook and eat it, and because it just tastes great. My hope is that you'll cook these dishes for your family and friends and that you'll think so too.

'For my family, sitting around the table together and filling ourselves with delicious food was a way of life.'

MENU 1

*Poireaux à la
vinaigrette de truffe*

BABY LEEKS WITH TRUFFLE
VINAIGRETTE

(see page 36)

*Rôti de porc aux pruneaux
façon mère Badet*

POT-ROASTED PORK WITH
PRUNES MOTHER BADET'S WAY

(see page 128)

SERVED WITH

*Haricots verts aux beurre
de morilles*

GREEN BEANS WITH
MOREL BUTTER

(see page 144)

Crème brûlée

VANILLA BEAN
CREME BRULEE

(see page 172)

MENU 2

Terrine de lapin

RABBIT TERRINE

(see page 35)

*Whiting en papillote et légumes
parfumés à l'estragon*

PAPILLOTE OF WHITING
AND TARRAGON-SCENTED
VEGETABLES

(see page 91)

Îles flottantes

FLOATING ISLANDS

(see page 186)

MENU 3

*Salade de concombres
à la crème fraîche*

CUCUMBER SALAD WITH
CRÈME FRAICHE DRESSING

(see page 10)

Gratin d'endives au jambon

BAKED WITLOF AND HAM GRATIN

(see page 134)

Tarte tatin de Maman

UPSIDE DOWN CARAMELISED
APPLE TART

(see page 168)

MENU 4

Choucroute de la mer

SEAFOOD CHOUCROUTE

(see page 72)

Sole meunière

FLOUNDER WITH LEMON
BUTTER SAUCE

(see page 88)

SERVED WITH

Flan de courgettes

ZUCCHINI FLANS

(see page 145)

*Soupe de fruits rouges et
son sorbet au yaourt*

BERRY SOUP WITH
YOGHURT SORBET

(see page 204)

MENU 5

Soupe vichysoisse
LEEK AND POTATO SOUP

(serve chilled, see page 48)

Côtes de porc Dijonnaise
PORK CUTLETS WITH CREAMY MUSTARD SAUCE

(see page 132)

SERVED WITH

FRESH TAGLIATELLE

Pithiviers
ALMOND TORTE

(see page 201)

MENU 6

Boudin de St Jacques au bisques de crustaces
SCALLOP BOUDIN WITH CRAB BISQUE SAUCE

(see page 78)

Carré d'agneau persillé
HERB-CRUSTED RACK OF LAMB

(see page 138)

SERVED WITH

Tomates à la Provençale
ROASTED TOMATOES WITH THYME

(see page 144)

Tarte au citron meringuée
LEMON MERINGUE TART

(see page 175)

MENU 7

*Cassolettes de moules
au safran*
MUSSEL AND SAFFRON PIES

(see page 38)

Steak au poivre
STEAK WITH
PEPPERCORN SAUCE

(see page 106)

SERVED WITH

Pommes dauphines
POTATO CROQUETTES

(see page 145)

Pêche Melba
PEACH MELBA

(see page 176)

MENU 8

*Salade de truite fumée,
pommes de terre nouvelles
et cresson*
SMOKED RAINBOW TROUT,
KIPFLER POTATO AND
WATERCRESS SALAD

(see page 20)

Pot-au-feu
POACHED BEEF IN BROTH

(see page 114)

Poires Belle Hélène
POACHED PEARS WITH
CHOCOLATE SAUCE

(see page 182)

SALADS & ENTREES

Salade de concombre à la crème fraîche
CUCUMBER SALAD WITH CREME FRAICHE DRESSING

My mum used to make this salad for me when I was a kid and I could never stop eating it. I loved the way the cucumber was cut into ribbons and how you could dunk your bread into the lovely creamy dressing at the end. I still do.

2 large telegraph cucumbers (about 670 g each)
sea salt
75 g creme fraiche or sour cream
3 teaspoons French Dijon mustard (see page 208)
3 teaspoons white-wine vinegar
freshly ground black pepper
2 teaspoons chopped dill, plus dill sprigs to serve

1 Peel the cucumbers, cut in half lengthways, then continue peeling the flesh into long thin ribbons with the vegetable peeler until you reach the seed core. Discard the seed core and place the cucumber in a colander sitting over a bowl. Sprinkle 1½ tablespoons salt over the cucumber, toss to mix well, then leave to stand for 10 minutes to release the liquid. Rinse the cucumber very well, gently squeeze dry and place in a bowl.

2 Combine the creme fraiche, mustard and vinegar in a bowl. Add to the cucumber along with the chopped dill and season to taste with salt and pepper. Toss to combine well, then scatter with dill sprigs and serve immediately.

Serves 4 as an accompaniment

Salade piémontaise
FRENCH-STYLE POTATO SALAD

This was one of the salads I learned how to make when I started working with my dad in his restaurant in Saint-Nazaire. It's a port town with a boat-building industry on the Atlantic coast and our clientele were mostly workers. This was a hearty lunch for them – with all that ham, egg and tomato we would serve it as a meal-in-itself, but you could also offer it as a side dish.

600 g kipfler potatoes, scrubbed
4 eggs
4 firm tomatoes, cored, halved widthways, seeded and
    cut into 1 cm pieces
1 × 200 g piece ham, cut into 1 cm pieces
5 cornichons (see page 208), thinly sliced lengthways
¼ cup finely chopped curly parsley
125 ml Mayonnaise (see page 23)

1   Place the potatoes in a large saucepan of lightly salted water, bring to the boil over high heat, then reduce the heat to medium and simmer for 20 minutes or until the potatoes are tender but still firm and not falling apart. Drain, then when cool enough to handle, peel and cut into large pieces.

2   Meanwhile, place the eggs in a small saucepan, cover with cold water and bring to the boil over medium heat. Cook for 6 minutes, then drain and refresh in cold water. Carefully shell the eggs, cut into quarters and set aside.

3   Place the potato, egg, tomato, ham and cornichons in a large bowl and toss gently to combine. Add the parsley and enough mayonnaise to just coat the other ingredients, then toss gently to combine. Serve.

Serves 4–6 as a light meal or accompaniment

Salade d'endive aux noix et Roquefort
WITLOF, WALNUT AND ROQUEFORT SALAD

Here's another classic combination that just works on every level – it's got bitter-ish leaves, pears for sweetness, a salty tang from the Roquefort, the crunch of walnuts and that savoury hazelnut dressing. I think of it as a cheeseboard whipped up into a salad; crusty baguette makes it perfect.

20 g unsalted butter
75 g walnuts
4 witlof
200 g mixed salad leaves, washed and dried
1 firm ripe pear
150 g Roquefort cheese, crumbled
¼ bunch chives, cut into 4 cm lengths
60 ml Hazelnut Vinaigrette (see page 22)

1   Melt the butter in a small frying pan over medium heat. When the butter starts to foam, add the walnuts and shake for 4–5 minutes or until they are toasted and glossy. Drain on paper towel.

2   Just before serving, remove the outermost leaves from the witlof, trim the bases and separate the rest of the leaves into a bowl. (Do this just before serving or the ends of the witlof will become brown.) Add the salad leaves and toss gently to combine.

3   Halve and core the pear, then cut into thin slivers. Scatter the pear, cheese, walnuts and chives over the salad. Pour enough hazelnut vinaigrette over the salad to just coat the leaves, then use your hands to gently combine. Serve immediately.

Serves 4–6 as an entree

Salade niçoise
NICOISE SALAD

For me the most important thing about nicoise salad is to use the very freshest tuna I can lay my hands on. And then to really only sear it so it's still quite rare in the middle. If you think you'll be tempted to cook tuna all the way through, then use a good-quality tinned tuna in oil instead – the salad will be just as delicious but in a slightly different way.

4 × 100 g tuna steaks
200 g small green beans, trimmed
table salt
12 small kipfler potatoes, scrubbed
4 eggs
30 nicoise or other small black olives, pitted
12 cherry tomatoes, halved
12 fillets salted anchovies (see page 208),
    rinsed well and halved lengthways
8 basil leaves, torn if large
1 tablespoon balsamic vinegar
90 ml olive oil
sea salt and freshly ground black pepper

1   Remove the tuna from the refrigerator 30 minutes before cooking.

2   Cook the beans in a saucepan of boiling salted water for 2 minutes or until tender but still firm to the bite. Drain and refresh under cold running water.

3   Meanwhile, steam the potatoes over a pan of simmering water for 15 minutes or until tender. When cool enough to handle, peel and cut into 2 cm thick slices.

4   Place the eggs in a small saucepan, cover with cold water and bring to the boil over medium heat. Once the water comes to the boil, cook for another 8 minutes for hard-boiled, then drain and refresh in cold water. Carefully shell the eggs, cut into quarters and set aside.

5   Place the beans, potato, olives, tomato, anchovies and basil in a bowl. Add the vinegar and 60 ml of the olive oil, then season to taste with salt and pepper and toss to combine.

6   Heat the remaining olive oil in a large frying pan over high heat. Season the tuna with salt and pepper to taste, then, when the pan is very hot, cook the tuna for 30 seconds on each side or until just golden but still rare in the middle. Remove from the heat and set aside.

7   To serve, divide the salad among 4 plates, top with a piece of tuna cut in half on the diagonal and scatter with the boiled egg.

Serves 4 as an entree or light meal

Salade de foies de volaille et lardons
CHICKEN LIVER, FRISEE AND SPECK SALAD

To be really honest, I'm not a huge liver fan and this is one of the only ways I truly enjoy eating it: that combination of smoky speck and rich, lean liver is simply one of the best there is. This dish makes a great warm salad to serve in winter. If you prefer, you can use poached eggs on top instead of the soft-boiled ones – when you do that, the yolk oozes all through the leaves and makes them just delicious.

4 eggs
300 g fresh chicken livers
2 tablespoons vegetable oil
20 g unsalted butter
1 × 200 g piece speck (see page 208), cut into
    3 cm × 1 cm strips (lardons, see page 208)
sea salt and freshly ground black pepper
2 tablespoons raspberry vinegar
¼ cup finely chopped curly parsley
300 g frisee, dark-green outer leaves removed, pale-yellow
    inner leaves picked, washed and dried
100 ml Raspberry Vinaigrette (see page 22)
50 g pine nuts, toasted (see page 209)
¼ bunch chives, cut into 4 cm lengths

1 Place the eggs in a small saucepan, cover with cold water and bring to the boil over medium heat. Boil for 2 minutes for soft-boiled, then drain and refresh in cold water. Carefully shell the eggs and set aside.

2 Remove any blood vessels, green-tinged parts and fat from the livers. Rinse well, then pat dry with paper towel.

3 Heat the oil and butter in a heavy-based frying pan over high heat. Add the speck and cook for 5 minutes or until golden. Remove with a slotted spoon, leaving as much fat in the pan as possible, and set aside.

4 Season the livers with salt and pepper. Add the livers to the hot pan and cook for 1 minute on each side or until golden but still pink in the centre. Add the vinegar and scrape the base of the pan to remove any cooked-on bits, then stir in the parsley and remove from the heat.

5 Place the frisee in a large bowl. Add the raspberry vinaigrette and toss gently to combine, then add the speck and liver mixture.

6 To serve, divide the salad among serving plates. Cut or gently tear the soft-boiled eggs in half and place on top, then scatter with the pine nuts and chives and serve immediately.

Serves 4 as an entree

Salade de truite fumée, pommes de terre nouvelles et cresson

SMOKED RAINBOW TROUT, KIPFLER POTATO AND WATERCRESS SALAD

I created this refreshing salad when I was putting together the spring menu for my restaurant, L'étoile, in 2009. I only wanted to feature one salad and really, I wasn't completely confident this one would be very popular. But it turned out to be a menu bestseller! The flavours are wonderful together (crisp apple, potato and lush smoky trout) and, as a bonus, it's super-easy to make.

300 g kipfler potatoes, scrubbed
2 large handfuls watercress, picked (about 180 g)
ice cubes
1 × 400 g hot-smoked rainbow trout
1 granny smith apple
1 bunch chives, cut into 3 cm lengths
½ lemon
extra virgin olive oil, for drizzling
sea salt and freshly ground black pepper
100 g creme fraiche or sour cream
3 teaspoons French Dijon mustard (see page 208)
lemon cheeks (optional), to serve

1 Cook the potatoes in a saucepan of boiling salted water for 20 minutes or until just tender, then drain. When the potatoes are cool enough to handle, peel and cut into 1 cm thick slices.

2 Meanwhile, place the watercress in a bowl of iced water for 10 minutes. Drain well.

3 Remove the trout skin, then remove the fillets from the bone, discarding the skin and bones. Flake the fillets into large pieces and place in a bowl, removing any small bones as you go.

4 Cut the unpeeled apple into matchsticks, then add to the trout along with the watercress and chives. Add a squeeze of lemon juice and a drizzle of olive oil, then season to taste with salt and pepper. Toss gently to combine.

5 Combine the creme fraiche and mustard in a large bowl and season to taste with salt and pepper. Add the potato and toss to combine.

6 To serve, divide the potato mixture among 4 plates (use small metal rings as a guide if you wish), then top with the trout salad and place a lemon cheek on the side, if desired.

Serves 4 as an entree or light meal

Vinaigrette
FRENCH DRESSING

1 teaspoon French Dijon mustard (see page 208)
60 ml red-wine vinegar
sea salt and freshly ground black pepper
200 ml olive oil

Place the mustard, vinegar and salt and pepper to taste in a bowl and whisk to combine well. Whisking continuously, gradually add the oil in a thin steady stream until emulsified.

Makes 260 ml

TIPS AND TRICKS

To make an emulsified dressing, you must whisk the acidic component (vinegar or lemon juice), mustard (if using) and the salt and pepper first. Salt doesn't dissolve in oil so must be dissolved in the vinegar. Once this is done, slowly whisk in the oil until emulsified.

It is handy to keep the dressing in a small screw-top jar in the refrigerator for up to 1 week. When needed, just shake the jar to emulsify again.

Vinaigrette au citron
LEMON DRESSING

60 ml lemon juice
150 ml olive oil
sea salt and freshly ground black pepper

Place all the ingredients in a small screw-top jar, seal and shake until well combined.

Makes 210 ml

Vinaigrette à la framboise
RASPBERRY VINAIGRETTE

50 ml raspberry vinegar
100 ml vegetable oil
50 ml olive oil
sea salt and freshly ground black pepper

Place all the ingredients in a small screw-top jar, seal and shake until well combined.

Makes 200 ml

Vinaigrette de noix ou noisette
WALNUT OR HAZELNUT VINAIGRETTE

1 teaspoon French Dijon mustard (see page 208)
50 ml white-wine vinegar
sea salt and freshly ground black pepper
50 ml vegetable oil
100 ml walnut or hazelnut oil

Place the mustard, vinegar and salt and pepper to taste in a bowl and whisk to combine well. Whisking continuously, gradually add the oil in a thin steady stream until emulsified.

Makes 200 ml

Mayonnaise

MAYONNAISE

1 egg yolk, at room temperature
1½ tablespoons French Dijon mustard (see page 208)
sea salt and freshly ground white pepper
250 ml grapeseed oil
1 teaspoon lemon juice, or to taste
boiling water (optional)

Place the egg yolk, mustard and a pinch each of salt and pepper in a bowl and whisk to combine well. Place the bowl on a kitchen cloth to help stabilise it as you whisk. Whisking continuously, add the oil, drop by drop at first, then in a slow, steady stream until the mixture is thick and emulsified. Whisk in the lemon juice and adjust the seasoning. If the mayonnaise is too thick, whisk in a little boiling water.

Makes about 250 ml

Aïoli

AIOLI

1 small brushed potato such as sebago
    (about 125 g), scrubbed
5 cloves garlic, peeled
sea salt
2 egg yolks, at room temperature
1 teaspoon lemon juice, or to taste
250 ml olive oil
pinch of cayenne pepper

Preheat the oven to 200°C. Prick the potato with a fork, then bake it directly on an oven rack for 35–40 minutes or until tender. When cool enough to handle, scoop out the flesh and discard the skin.

Place the garlic and a large pinch of salt in a mortar and pound with a pestle until a paste forms. Transfer to a food processor. Add the egg yolks, lemon juice and 30 g of the potato and process until smooth. With the motor running, gradually add the oil, drop by drop at first, and then in a slow, steady stream until the mixture is thick and emulsified. Season to taste with salt, cayenne pepper and a little more lemon juice if needed.

Makes about 375 ml

Rouille

GARLIC AND ROASTED CAPSICUM MAYONNAISE

1 small brushed potato such as sebago
    (about 125 g), scrubbed
1 red capsicum (pepper)
5 cloves garlic, peeled
sea salt
2 egg yolks, at room temperature
1 teaspoon lemon juice, or to taste
pinch of saffron threads
250 ml olive oil
pinch of cayenne pepper

Preheat the oven to 200°C.

Prick the potato all over with a fork, then bake it directly on an oven rack for 35–40 minutes or until tender. When cool enough to handle, scoop out the flesh and discard the skin.

Meanwhile, roast the capsicum directly on a gas flame until the skin blackens and blisters. (Alternatively, grill under a hot griller turning until the skin blackens and blisters.) Transfer to a bowl, cover with plastic film and leave for 10 minutes or until cool enough to handle. Peel the capsicum, then discard the seeds and chop the flesh.

Place the garlic and a large pinch of salt in a mortar and pound with a pestle until a paste forms. Transfer the garlic paste to a food processor, then add the egg yolks, capsicum, lemon juice, saffron threads and 30 g of the potato and process until smooth. With the motor running, gradually add the oil, drop by drop at first, and then in a slow steady stream until the mixture is thick and emulsified. Season to taste with salt, the cayenne pepper and a little more lemon juice if needed.

Makes about 430 ml

Rillettes de porc
PORK RILLETTES

Rillettes is a type of French charcuterie, where meat such as pork, rabbit or duck is salted and slowly cooked in fat until it is tender and can be shredded easily. The mixture is then cooled and served spread on fresh bread or toast. I find rillettes can be far too fatty sometimes, so when I make mine I include a bit of lean meat in the mix (such as pork loin). You actually don't need to use the highest quality of pork for this rustic recipe. For rabbit rillettes, substitute the pork shoulder with the boned meat from a two kilogram rabbit.

500 g boned pork shoulder, cut into 2.5 cm pieces
1 × 125 g piece pork loin, cut into 2.5 cm pieces
20 g coarse sea salt
1 juniper berry
5 black peppercorns
1 clove
1 bay leaf
2 sprigs thyme
375 g pork back fat (see page 208), cut into 1 cm pieces
freshly ground black pepper

1   Place the pork shoulder and loin in a large bowl. Place the salt, juniper berry, peppercorns and clove in a mortar and pound with a pestle until finely ground. Add the spice mix to the pork, along with the bay leaf and thyme, then combine well. Cover with plastic film and refrigerate for 24 hours.

2   Place 50 g of the back fat in a large heavy-based frying pan and cook over low heat until melted. Increase the heat to high, then, working in batches, cook the marinated pork for 5 minutes or until browned all over. Remove the pork from the pan and place in an enamelled cast-iron or other heavy-based casserole with the remaining back fat and enough water to come two-thirds of the way up the pork (about 310 ml). Cook over very low heat, stirring regularly, for 3½–4 hours or until the meat is very tender and almost falling apart. Drain the meat in a colander placed over a large jug and reserve the fat. Set the fat aside to cool.

3   Using a fork or your fingers, shred the pork and transfer to a large bowl, then add the cooled fat and combine well. Cover with plastic film and refrigerate for 30 minutes, then stir to combine again, making sure the fat and the meat do not separate. Check the seasoning and adjust with extra salt and pepper if necessary. Spoon the mixture into a 650 ml capacity terrine mould or four 150 ml capacity ramekins. Smooth the tops, then cover with plastic film and refrigerate for 2 days before serving.

Serves 10–12 as an entree

Céleri rémoulade
CELERIAC REMOULADE

Serve this as an entree, family-style, where everyone gets to help themselves from a big bowl; I wouldn't bother to plate this up. Oh, and remoulade makes a great picnic dish too, maybe with my Cucumber Salad with Creme Fraiche Dressing (see page 10) and some cold roast chicken (see page 150) alongside.

400 g (about 1 small head) celeriac
2 granny smith apples
150 ml Mayonnaise (see page 23)
⅓ cup chopped flat-leaf parsley
juice of ½ lemon, or to taste
sea salt and freshly ground black pepper

1   Trim, wash, peel and quarter the celeriac and apples. Coarsely grate the celeriac and apples, using the medium holes on your grater (or a food processor grater attachment), then place in a bowl.

2   Stir the mayonnaise into the celeriac and apple, then stir in the parsley and lemon juice and season to taste with salt and pepper. Serve.

Serves 4–6

Oeufs en cocotte Florentine
CODDLED EGGS WITH SPINACH

The loose cooking time here (7–12 minutes) is because everyone's oven cooks slightly differently – some are hotter, some cooler. The trick is to have the cream mixture bubbling hot and the eggs only just set in the middle, so you have to watch closely and use your judgement. You can change the flavours easily – add ham or salami, for example, or replace the spinach with your favourite green vegetable.

1½ tablespoons olive oil
150 g baby spinach, picked and washed
sea salt and freshly ground black pepper
15 g unsalted butter, melted
freshly grated nutmeg, to taste
160 ml pouring cream
8 very fresh eggs

1   Preheat the oven to 180°C.

2   Heat the oil in a frying pan over medium–high heat. Add the spinach and toss for 1–2 minutes or until just wilted. Season to taste with salt and pepper and transfer to a colander. Press down on the spinach with the back of a large spoon (or use your hands) to remove as much excess liquid as possible.

3   Brush the inside of four shallow 250 ml capacity ramekins or gratin dishes with the melted butter. Sprinkle a little nutmeg, salt and pepper into each ramekin, then place them in a deep roasting pan. Divide the spinach among the ramekins, then pour 2 tablespoons of the cream into each one. Carefully crack 2 eggs into each ramekin. Pour enough boiling water into the pan to come halfway up the sides of the ramekins.

4   Bake the eggs for 7–12 minutes or until the whites are just set and the yolks are still runny. Remember, when you take the eggs out of the water bath, they will continue to cook. If the eggs are still a little runny for your liking, leave the ramekins to stand for 3–4 minutes. Season with a little pepper, then serve.

Serves 4 as a light meal

Quiche Lorraine de ma maman
MY MUM'S QUICHE LORRAINE

This is another of Mum's classic recipes. A traditional quiche Lorraine is a great simple dish and I think it should be kept that way. I'm not a huge fan of the trend to throw everything into a quiche, so I think this recipe is fantastic – not too eggy, and the bacon flavour really comes through. Please eat it warm, when the taste and texture are perfect. In my opinion, cold quiche is just plain awful.

½ quantity Shortcrust Pastry (see page 206)
plain flour, for dusting
1 tablespoon vegetable oil
1 × 100 g piece speck, cut into 3 cm × 1 cm strips
    (lardons, see page 209)
1 egg
1 egg yolk
100 ml milk
100 ml pouring cream
pinch of freshly grated nutmeg
sea salt and freshly ground black pepper
50 g gruyerè or emmenthal cheese, grated
thyme leaves (optional), to serve

1   Roll out the pastry on a lightly floured surface, then use to line the base and side of a 20 cm ceramic quiche dish or tart tin with a removable base. Use a small sharp knife to trim off the excess pastry. Refrigerate for 30 minutes.

2   Preheat the oven to 190°C.

3   Line the pastry shell with baking paper, then fill with pastry weights, dried beans or rice and bake for 15 minutes. Remove the paper and weights, then reduce the oven temperature to 180°C and bake the pastry for another 5 minutes or until it is dry and light golden. Remove from the oven and leave to stand until cool.

4   Meanwhile, heat the oil in a frying pan over medium heat. Add the speck and cook, stirring often, for 5 minutes or until golden. Drain on paper towel.

5   Place the egg, yolk, milk, cream, nutmeg and salt and pepper to taste in a bowl and whisk to combine. Stir in the cheese and speck, then pour the mixture into the pastry shell and bake for 20 minutes or until just set. Scatter with thyme leaves, if desired, and serve warm.

Serves 4–6 as a light meal

Pissaladière
ONION, CAPSICUM AND ANCHOVY TART

This is the famous tart that hails from Nice. They don't put capsicum in it there, but I think the capsicum brings a bit of extra life to the dish. Use marinated anchovies if you don't like (or can't get) the salted ones, and as with any recipe using puff pastry, I recommend using a decent butter-based one. It makes all the difference.

2 sheets ready-rolled butter puff pastry, thawed
100 ml olive oil
4 onions, sliced
1 tablespoon chopped thyme, plus extra (optional), to serve
sea salt
1 large red capsicum (pepper)
42 kalamata olives, pitted and halved
20 anchovies (see page 208), halved lengthways

1   Preheat the oven to 190°C and line two baking trays with baking paper.

2   Using a dinner plate as a guide, cut out two 25 cm rounds of pastry and place one on each baking tray. Prick the pastry all over with a fork, then put another layer of baking paper and another baking tray over the top – this stops the pastry from rising unevenly. Bake for 20 minutes or until golden and crisp.

3   Meanwhile, heat the olive oil a large heavy-based saucepan over medium heat. Add the onion, thyme and a pinch of salt and combine well. Reduce the heat to very low and cook, stirring often to prevent the onion catching on the base, for 1 hour or until caramelised.

4   Place the capsicum directly over a low gas flame and cook on all sides until blackened (or grill under a hot griller). Transfer the capsicum to a bowl, cover with plastic film and leave to stand until cool enough to handle. Peel the capsicum and discard the seeds and white membrane. Cut the flesh into thin strips and set aside.

5   Place half of the onion in a thick layer over each of the pastry bases, then place the capsicum and anchovy halves in a criss-cross pattern over the top. Place an olive half in between the capsicum and anchovy, scatter with extra thyme, if desired, and serve.

Serves 8 as a light meal

Cassolette de ris de veau aux morilles
SWEETBREAD AND MOREL PIES

I once fed these pies to people who didn't know there were sweetbreads inside, and they loved them. If I'd told them about the contents first I suspect they wouldn't have tried them. In France, sweetbreads are very expensive but in Australia I've heard of people giving them to their cats – sacrilege! They have the best texture, especially when they're caramelised on the outside and soft and creamy on the inside.

10 g dried morel mushrooms (see page 209)
100 ml hot water
250 g veal sweetbreads (order from
    your butcher)
5 black peppercorns
½ onion
1 sprig thyme
1 bay leaf
pinch of coarse sea salt
sea salt and freshly ground black pepper
1½ tablespoons vegetable oil

40 g unsalted butter
200 g button mushrooms, trimmed
    and quartered
2 eschalots, finely chopped
2 cloves garlic, finely chopped
150 ml White Chicken Stock (see page 46)
100 ml pouring cream
2 tablespoons chopped curly parsley
1 sheet ready-rolled butter puff
    pastry, thawed
1 egg yolk

1 Place the dried morels and hot water in a small bowl and leave for 15 minutes. Drain the morels, then strain and reserve the soaking liquid. Rinse the morels again to remove any excess grit, then coarsely chop.

2 Meanwhile, place the sweetbreads, peppercorns, onion, thyme, bay leaf and salt in a saucepan. Cover with cold water and bring to the boil over medium heat. Remove the pan from the heat immediately and leave to stand for 5 minutes. (It is important not to overcook the sweetbreads or they will toughen.) Drain the sweetbreads on paper towel and refrigerate until cold. Peel the sweetbreads, remove any fat and season to taste with salt and pepper.

3 Heat the oil and 20 g of the butter in a frying pan over medium heat. When the butter starts to foam, add the sweetbreads and cook on each side for 1–2 minutes or until just golden. Remove from the pan and set aside. Add the remaining butter to the pan and, when it starts to foam, cook the button mushrooms for 5 minutes or until golden. Add the morels, eschalot and garlic and stir for another 2–3 minutes or until fragrant. Add the stock and the morel soaking water (leave the last gritty soaking water behind). Simmer for 8 minutes or until reduced by half. Add the cream and simmer until reduced by half again. Season to taste with salt and pepper, stir in the parsley, then remove from the heat and leave to stand until cool.

4 Preheat the oven to 200°C.

5 Cut the sweetbreads into bite-sized pieces and divide among four 150 ml capacity ramekins (mine are 9 cm). Pour the mushroom sauce over the top.

6 Using a pastry cutter, cut out four 12 cm rounds of puff pastry and score in a criss-cross pattern, taking care not to cut all the way through. Place over the top of the ramekins, pressing down the sides firmly to seal well. Place on a baking tray, brush the tops with the egg yolk and, using a wooden skewer or small knife, make a small hole in the centre to allow steam to escape. Bake the pies for 12 minutes or until the pastry is puffed, golden and crisp. Serve.

Serves 4 as an entree or light meal

Terrine de lapin
RABBIT TERRINE

I can't go past a terrine. It's very French and there's nothing better to get a meal started. My uncle makes charcuterie in France and I recently returned there to spend a few weeks with him learning the craft. It is amazing to see whole pigs, chickens and rabbits delivered in the morning and then watch as they are transformed into delicious sausages, andouillettes (coarse tripe sausage), terrines and pates. For me, it's like a magic show! In France you can buy caul fat in rolls like pastry, but in Australia you'll need to order it in advance from a good-quality butcher.

1 × 2.3 kg farmed white rabbit, boned, fat
    and sinew trimmed (or ask your butcher
    to do this – you need 750 g meat)
500 g pork shoulder
750 g pork back fat (see page 208)
1 bay leaf
1 tablespoon chopped thyme
sea salt and freshly ground black pepper
pinch of quatre-épices (see page 209)
50 ml port

50 ml brandy
80 ml olive oil
2 eschalots, finely chopped
1 clove garlic, finely chopped
1 egg
⅓ cup finely chopped curly parsley
200 g caul fat (see page 208, optional)
toasted sourdough bread, French Dijon
    mustard (see page 208) and cornichons
    (see page 208), to serve

1 Cut the rabbit meat into 1–2 cm pieces and place in a large bowl. Using the coarse plate on a grinder, mince the pork shoulder and back fat and add to the rabbit meat (or ask your kind butcher to do this for you). Add the bay leaf, thyme, 2 tablespoons salt, 3 teaspoons pepper, quatre-épices, port and brandy and combine well, then cover and refrigerate overnight.

2 Preheat the oven to 140°C.

3 Heat the olive oil in a small frying pan over low heat. Add the eschalot and garlic and stir for 4–5 minutes or until soft but not coloured. Remove from the heat and set aside to cool.

4 Add the egg, parsley and cooled onion and garlic to the rabbit mixture. Using very clean hands, combine the mixture very well until the fat is sticky and the mixture looks cohesive. (This step is important in making sure the terrine is not crumbly once cooked.) Remove the bay leaf.

5 Rinse the caul fat (if using) under cold running water, then drain well. Use to line a 2 litre capacity terrine mould in a single layer without any overlaps. (Alternatively, line the base and sides of the terrine mould with baking paper.) Spoon the mixture into the terrine mould and fold over the caul fat or baking paper to cover the top. Press down firmly to remove any air pockets.

6 Place the terrine mould in a deep roasting pan and pour in enough boiling water to come halfway up the sides. Bake the terrine for 1½–2 hours or until the internal temperature of the terrine reaches 60°C on a meat thermometer. Carefully remove the roasting pan from the oven, then remove the terrine mould and pour off the excess fat. Place a smaller tin over the top of the terrine and fill with bricks or tinned food to weight the terrine down. Leave to cool, then refrigerate overnight.

7 Just before serving, cut the terrine into slices. Serve with toasted sourdough bread, Dijon mustard and cornichons.

Serves 12 as an entree

Poireaux à la vinaigrette de truffe
BABY LEEKS WITH TRUFFLE VINAIGRETTE

This classic was 'invented' by Paul Bocuse in the 1970s. The combination is unbeatable: leeks, truffle and tomatoes. Mmm. I love baby leeks; they look so beautiful. But, if you can't get them, or you prefer larger leeks, use those instead. You will need to increase the cooking time for larger leeks but that's easily done – simply keep cooking them until they are tender.

12 baby thumb-sized leeks, green tops and roots ends
    trimmed, washed well and cut into 8 cm lengths
table salt
ice cubes
2 roma (plum) tomatoes, peeled (see page 209), seeded
    and finely chopped
2 tablespoons finely chopped chives
1 tablespoon olive oil
sea salt and freshly ground black pepper
100 ml French Dressing (see page 22)
20 g black truffle, very thinly shaved
small handful of micro-cress and frisee (optional), to serve

1   Cook the leeks in a pan of lightly salted boiling water until tender, then drain and refresh in iced water. Drain well, gently squeezing excess water out of the leeks, then pat dry.

2   Place the tomato, chives and olive oil in a bowl, then season to taste with salt and pepper and toss gently to combine.

3   Blend the dressing and truffle in a blender or small food processor until amalgamated.

4   To serve, cut the leeks in half lengthways and divide among plates or place on a large serving plate. Place the tomato and chive mixture on one end of the leeks and the micro-cress and frisee (if using) on the other end, and drizzle with the truffle vinaigrette.

Serves 4 as an entree

Cassolettes de moules au safran
MUSSEL AND SAFFRON PIES

In Brittany we have amazing mussels called bouchots, which are very small but incredibly sweet and juicy. In Australia, I use farmed black mussels from South Australia both at home and in the restaurant and find them to be exceptionally good. I've visited the farms and was really impressed by their methods and high standards. This pie, with saffron and cream for luxury and leek for sweetness, is a great way to serve mussels.

1 kg black mussels, scrubbed and bearded
100 ml dry white wine
1 eschalot, thinly sliced
1 clove garlic, bruised
1 sprig thyme
1 bay leaf
3 black peppercorns
100 ml White Chicken Stock (see page 46)
80 ml pouring cream
pinch of saffron threads

freshly ground black pepper
2 teaspoons unsalted butter
1½ tablespoons olive oil
1 small leek, white part only, cut
   into julienne (see page 209)
1 carrot, cut into julienne (see page 209)
1 sheet ready-rolled butter puff
   pastry, thawed
1 egg yolk

1   Discard any mussels with open or broken shells.

2   Place the wine, eschalot, garlic, thyme, bay leaf and peppercorns in a wide frying pan over high heat. Bring to the boil and simmer for 2 minutes. Add the mussels, then cover and shake the pan for 3–4 minutes or until the shells just open. Remove the mussels using a large slotted spoon as soon as the shells open or they will become tough – some will take longer to cook than others. Place the mussels in a colander sitting over a bowl, discarding any with unopened shells. Remove the meat from the shells, checking each one and removing any beard still attached to the meat. Strain the cooking liquor through a fine-mesh sieve over a bowl, leaving any grit behind in the pan. Set aside.

3   Place the chicken stock, cream, saffron and 50 ml of the reserved mussel liquor in a saucepan. Simmer over low heat for 6 minutes or until reduced by half. Season to taste with pepper, then remove from the heat and set aside to cool.

4   Meanwhile, heat the butter and olive oil in a heavy-based saucepan over low heat. Add the leek and carrot, then cover and cook for 6–8 minutes or until just tender.

5   Preheat the oven to 200°C.

6   Divide the leek and carrot mixture and mussels among four 150 ml capacity ramekins (mine are 9 cm in diameter) or pie dishes. Pour over the cooled sauce.

7   Using a pastry cutter, cut out four 12 cm rounds of puff pastry and place one over the top of each ramekin, pressing down the sides firmly to seal well. Cut 4 mussel shapes from the remaining pastry and place one on top of each pie. Place the ramekins on a baking tray, brush the pastry tops with egg yolk, and using a wooden skewer or small knife, make a small hole in the centre of each one to allow the steam to escape. Bake for 12 minutes or until the pastry is puffed, golden and crisp. Serve.

Serves 4 as an entree or light meal

Croque monsieur
CROQUE MONSIEUR

Did you know that if you put a sunny-side-up egg on top of one of these sandwiches it becomes a croque madame? Because this dish is so simple, it only really works if you use the best of ingredients. That means good-quality white sourdough bread, leg ham and best-quality gruyère cheese. It just won't be the same if you use shaved ham, cheddar and supermarket sliced bread.

4 slices leg ham
8 slices good-quality white bread,
    such as sourdough
1 × 300 g piece gruyère cheese
3 egg yolks
100 ml pouring cream
freshly ground black pepper
40 g unsalted butter, softened
green salad (optional), to serve

1   Preheat a griller to high and line a baking tray with baking paper.

2   Cut each slice of ham to match the size of the bread. Thinly slice 200 g of the gruyère and cut to match the size of the bread. Grate the remaining cheese and combine in a bowl with the egg yolks and cream, then season to taste with pepper.

3   Spread one side of each slice of bread with butter and place, buttered-side down, on a baking tray lined with baking paper. Top with a slice of gruyère, a slice of ham and another slice of gruyère. Top with the remaining bread slices and spread with the egg and cheese mixture, then grill under the griller until golden and bubbling. Serve immediately, with a green salad, if desired.

Serves 4

Cassolettes d'escargots à l'anis
SNAIL AND FENNEL PIES

Cooking and eating snails reminds me of my childhood in France. On rainy days, my grandmother would go out snail picking. She would fast the snails for one day and then cook them the next day. When I cook snails now, I think of her.

1 bulb fennel, trimmed, quartered and
    core removed
90 ml olive oil
60 g unsalted butter, chopped
1 carrot, cut into julienne (see page 209)
sea salt and freshly ground black pepper
2 eschalots, finely chopped
3 teaspoons fennel seeds
1 star anise
200 ml White Chicken Stock (see page 46)

150 ml pouring cream
24 tinned snails (see page 209), drained
2 cloves garlic, finely chopped
1½ tablespoons pastis (such as Pernod
    or Ricard)
2 tablespoons finely chopped curly parsley
1 sheet ready-rolled butter puff
    pastry, thawed
1 egg yolk

1   Using a mandoline, shave the fennel as thinly as possible.

2   Heat 1½ tablespoons of the oil and 20 g of the butter in a saucepan over low heat. Add the carrot and fennel, season to taste with salt and pepper, then cover and cook for 5 minutes or until tender. Remove from the heat.

3   Heat another 1½ tablespoons of the oil and 20 g butter in another saucepan over medium heat. Add the eschalot, fennel seeds and star anise and stir for 3–4 minutes or until the eschalot is soft but not coloured. Add the stock and cream and simmer for 5 minutes or until reduced by two-thirds. Remove the star anise, then puree the sauce in a blender until smooth. Strain through a fine-mesh sieve over a bowl and set aside to cool.

4   Pat the snails dry with paper towel, then season to taste with salt and pepper. Heat the remaining 1½ tablespoons oil and butter in a large frying pan over medium heat. Add the snails and stir for 4 minutes. Add the garlic and cook for another 2–3 minutes or until fragrant. Add the pastis, then carefully tilt the pan towards the flame to ignite the alcohol (or use a lighter if necessary). Once the flames have subsided, remove the pan from the heat.

5   Preheat the oven to 200°C.

6   Divide the carrot and fennel mixture among four 150 ml capacity ramekins (mine are 9 cm in diameter). Top with the snails, then pour over the sauce and scatter with the parsley.

7   Using a pastry cutter, cut out four 12 cm rounds of puff pastry and place over the top of the ramekins, pressing down the sides firmly to seal well. Place on a baking tray, brush the tops with the egg yolk and, using a wooden skewer or small knife, make a small hole in the centre to allow the steam to escape. Bake the pies for 12 minutes or until the pastry is puffed, golden and crisp. Serve.

Serves 4 as an entree or light meal

Oeufs mimosa
FRENCH-STYLE EGG MAYONNAISE

A mimosa is a type of flower and these eggs, which have their filling piped into them, do look rather flower-like and pretty. They are a great thing to give to kids, although be warned, they are likely to become addicted to them. This also makes a really simple but extremely tasty appetiser, especially in summer while your guests wait for the barbecued meat to cook.

6 eggs
2 teaspoons finely chopped chives
1 tablespoon finely chopped curly parsley
2½ tablespoons Mayonnaise (see page 23)
sea salt and freshly ground black pepper

1   Place the eggs in a small saucepan, cover with cold water and bring to the boil over medium heat. Once the water comes to the boil, cook for another 8 minutes for hard-boiled, then drain and refresh in cold water. Carefully shell the eggs and set aside to cool.

2   Using a large sharp knife, cut the eggs in half lengthways and carefully remove the yolks. Place the egg yolks in a small bowl and, using the back of a fork, mash until smooth. Add the parsley and mayonnaise and season to taste with salt and pepper. Spoon the mixture into a piping bag fitted with a 2 cm star-shaped nozzle and pipe the mixture into the hollow of the egg whites. Serve.

Serves 4 as an entree

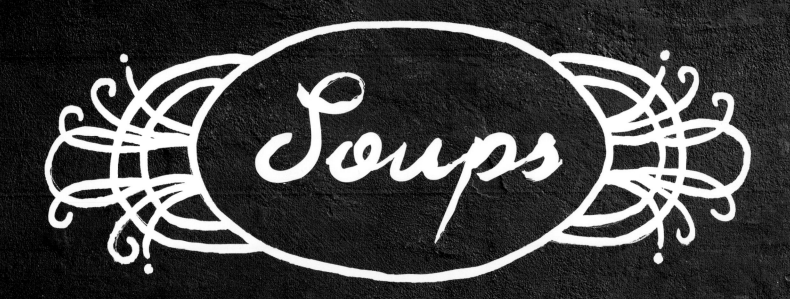

Fond blanc de volaille
WHITE CHICKEN STOCK

1 kg chicken bones, rinsed well
3 litres water
1 carrot, diced
1 onion, diced
1 small leek, white part only, diced
1 stalk celery, diced
1 clove garlic
1 bouquet garni (see page 208)

Place the chicken bones and water in a large saucepan or stockpot. Bring to the boil over medium heat, skimming any impurities from the surface. Add the carrot, onion, leek, celery, garlic and bouquet garni and return to the boil. Reduce the heat to low and simmer for 3 hours, skimming regularly.

Strain the stock through a fine-mesh sieve sitting over a large bowl and discard the solids. (To keep the stock as clear as possible, do not press on the vegetables when straining.) Cool to room temperature, then refrigerate until cold. The fat will solidify on top of the stock, making it easy to remove and discard. Refrigerate for up to 7 days or freeze for up to 3 months. (Freeze the stock in ice-cube trays so you can take out only as much as you need.)

Makes about 2 litres

TIPS AND TRICKS

To make a beautiful rich gravy to go with roast chicken, leave the fat in the stock after straining. Simmer 750 ml of the stock in a saucepan over medium heat for 20 minutes or until reduced by half, then whisk until emulsified.

A glaze (or glace) is an easy way to add a flavour boost to sauces. To make a glaze, strain the stock, then return it to a clean saucepan and simmer until reduced to one-fifth of its original volume. Cool and freeze in ice-cube trays and use within 3 months.

Fond brun de volaille
BROWN CHICKEN STOCK

1 kg chicken bones, rinsed well
1 carrot, diced
1 onion, diced
1 stalk celery, diced
100 g button mushrooms, quartered
500 ml dry white wine
2.5 litres water
1 clove garlic
1 bouquet garni (see page 208)
2 tomatoes, halved widthways

Preheat the oven to 200°C. Place the bones in a large roasting pan and roast for 30 minutes, stirring occasionally. Add the carrot, onion, celery and mushrooms, stir to combine well, then roast for another 30 minutes or until the vegetables are golden. Transfer the bones and vegetables to a large saucepan or stockpot and reserve the roasting pan.

Place the roasting pan over medium heat. Add the wine and scrape with a wooden spoon to remove any cooked-on bits. Pour the wine mixture over the bones, then add the water. Bring to the boil over high heat, then skim any impurities from the surface. Add the garlic, bouquet garni and tomato to the pan, reduce the heat to low and simmer for 4 hours, skimming the surface regularly.

Strain the stock through a fine-mesh sieve sitting over a large bowl. Discard the solids. (To keep the stock as clear as possible, do not press on the vegetables when straining.) Cool to room temperature, then refrigerate until cold. The fat will solidify on top of the stock, making it easy to discard. Refrigerate for up to 7 days or freeze for up to 3 months. (Freeze the stock in ice-cube trays so you can take out only as much as you need.)

Makes about 1.7 litres

Fond brun de veau
BROWN VEAL STOCK

1 kg veal bones
1 carrot, diced
1 onion, diced
1 stalk celery, diced
100 g button mushrooms, quartered
500 ml dry red wine
2.5 litres water
1 clove garlic
1 bouquet garni (see page 208)
2 tomatoes, halved widthways

Preheat the oven to 200°C. Place the bones in a large roasting pan and roast for 30 minutes or until well browned, stirring from time to time. Add the carrot, onion, celery and mushrooms and stir, then roast for another 30 minutes or until the vegetables are well browned. Transfer the vegetables and bones to a large saucepan or stockpot and reserve the roasting pan.

Place the roasting pan over medium heat. Add the wine and scrape with a wooden spoon to remove any cooked-on bits. Pour the wine mixture over the bones, then add the water. Bring to the boil over high heat and skim any impurities from the surface. Add the garlic, bouquet garni and tomato, then reduce the heat to low and simmer for 4 hours, skimming the surface regularly.

Strain the stock through a fine-mesh sieve sitting over a large bowl. Discard the solids. (To keep the stock as clear as possible, do not press on the vegetables when straining.) Cool to room temperature, then refrigerate until cold. The fat will solidify on top of the stock, making it easy to discard. Refrigerate for up to 7 days or freeze for up to 3 months. (Freeze the stock in ice-cube trays so you can take out only as much as you need.)

Makes about 1.7 litres

Fumet de poisson
FISH STOCK

1 kg white fish heads and bones, cleaned and washed
100 ml dry white wine
3 litres water
1 onion, diced
1 small leek, white part only, diced
1 small bulb fennel, diced
1 clove garlic
1 bouquet garni (see page 208)

Place the heads, bones and wine in a large saucepan or stockpot and bring to the boil over high heat. Add the water and return to the boil. Reduce the heat to low, then add the onion, leek, fennel, garlic and bouquet garni and simmer, skimming the surface regularly, for 20 minutes, then remove from the heat. Strain the stock through a fine-mesh sieve sitting over a large bowl and discard the solids. (To keep the stock as clear as possible, do not press on the vegetables when straining.) Cool to room temperature, then refrigerate for up to 7 days or freeze for up to 3 months. (Freeze the stock in ice-cube trays so you can take out only as much as you need.)

Makes about 2.75 litres

Nage de légumes
VEGETABLE STOCK

2 stalks celery, diced
2 leeks, white part only, diced
2 carrots, diced
1 onion, diced
2 cloves garlic
2 litres water
500 ml dry white wine
1 bouquet garni (see page 208)

Bring all the ingredients to the boil in a stockpot and skim any impurities from the surface. Reduce the heat to low and simmer for 2 hours, skimming regularly. Strain the stock through a fine-mesh sieve sitting over a bowl. Discard the solids. (To keep the stock as clear as possible, do not press on the vegetables when straining.) Cool to room temperature, then refrigerate for up to 7 days or freeze for up to 3 months. (Freeze the stock in ice-cube trays so you can take out only as much as you need.)

Makes about 1.25 litres

Soupe vichyssoise
LEEK AND POTATO SOUP

This is such a classic and – in my opinion – may be the best soup ever. Everyone loves it. And it is so versatile; you can savour it cold in summer or hot in winter. If you'd like to jazz it up a bit, there's a version where you stir oyster juice into cream then whip it and float it on the top. Yum!

50 g unsalted butter
300 g desiree potatoes, peeled, halved and thinly sliced
2 leeks (about 500 g), white part only, rinsed well,
    halved and thinly sliced
1 litre water
1 sprig thyme
1 bay leaf
100 g creme fraiche, plus extra to serve
sea salt and freshly ground white pepper
finely chopped chives (optional) and crusty
    bread, to serve

1   Melt the butter in a heavy-based saucepan over low heat. When the butter starts to foam, add the potato and cook for 5 minutes – you don't want it to take on any colour. Add the leek and stir for another 3 minutes or until just wilted. Add the water, then increase the heat to high and bring to the boil. Add the thyme and bay leaf. Simmer for 20 minutes or until the potato is tender when pierced with a knife. Remove the thyme and bay leaf.

2   Puree the soup in a blender until smooth. Leave the soup in the blender to stand until just warm. Add the creme fraiche and blend again until well combined. Season to taste with salt and pepper, then serve warm or refrigerate until cold.

3   To serve, divide among bowls, then scatter with chives (if using). Serve with crusty bread alongside, topped with a spoonful of creme fraiche.

Serves 4

Crème de champignons
CREAMY MUSHROOM SOUP

Mushroom soup is one of those easy, wintry soups that are just perfect for eating with crusty bread, preferably on the sofa and watching *My Kitchen Rules*! In general, I don't think any vegetable-based soup should take more than twenty minutes to cook – any longer and you just kill the flavour of the vegetables.

20 g unsalted butter
2 eschalots, finely chopped
500 g button mushrooms, wiped clean
100 ml dry white wine
1 litre White Chicken Stock (see page 46)
100 g creme fraiche
sea salt and freshly ground white pepper
extra virgin olive oil (optional), for drizzling

1   Melt the butter in a heavy-based saucepan over low heat. When the butter starts to foam, add the eschalot and stir for 4–5 minutes or until soft but not coloured. Add the mushrooms and stir for another 5 minutes.

2   Increase the heat to high, then add the wine and simmer for 5 minutes or until reduced by half. Add the stock, bring to the boil, then reduce the heat to low and simmer for 20 minutes.

3   Puree the soup in a blender until smooth, then stir in the creme fraiche and season to taste with salt and pepper. Drizzle with extra virgin olive oil, if desired. Serve.

Serves 4

Velouté d'asperges

CREAMY ASPARAGUS SOUP

Here's a ladies' favourite – especially if the guys are cooking it. Asparagus makes a soup that is elegant, silky and just plain sexy. If you want, you can just use the asparagus stalks here and save the tips for a salad garnish or to serve with Hollandaise Sauce (see page 97). That's what I call cooking two birds with one stove!

500 g white or green asparagus, unpeeled, cut into 3 cm pieces
200 g desiree potato (about 1), cut into 3 cm pieces
1.5 litres White Chicken Stock (see page 46)
200 ml pouring cream
sea salt and freshly ground white or black pepper
crusty bread (optional), to serve

1   Place the asparagus, potato and stock in a saucepan and bring to the boil over medium heat. Reduce the heat to low and simmer for 20 minutes or until the potato is tender.

2   Puree the soup in a blender until smooth. Strain through a fine-mesh sieve into a clean pan, pushing with the bottom of a ladle to extract as much liquid as possible. Simmer over low heat for 15 minutes or until reduced by one-third. Add the cream, then season to taste with salt and pepper. Simmer the soup for another 3–4 minutes or until slightly reduced and thickened. Season with extra pepper, if desired, and serve with crusty bread.

Serves 4

Crème de chou-fleur de maman
MY MUM'S CAULIFLOWER SOUP

Cauliflower soup stirs up strong childhood memories for me; my mum would put bowls of this down in front of us kids and we wouldn't come up for air until every last bit was finished. I just love cauliflower as a vegetable and every time I eat it, it brings a smile to my face. It reminds me of my mum.

40 g unsalted butter
1 small head cauliflower (about 1 kg), core removed,
    cut into small florets
1 litre White Chicken Stock (see page 46)
100 g creme fraiche
sea salt and freshly ground white pepper

1   Melt the butter in a heavy-based saucepan over medium heat. When the butter starts to foam, add the cauliflower and stir for 3–4 minutes – you do not want it to take on any colour. Add the stock, bring to the boil, then reduce the heat to low and simmer for 20 minutes or until the cauliflower is very tender.

2   Puree the soup in a blender until smooth. Whisk in the creme fraiche, then season to taste with salt and pepper. Serve.

Serves 4

Crème de petits pois
PEA SOUP

Let me come clean – I don't think there is anything wrong with using frozen peas here. Peas are one of the few vegetables that do not suffer at all from being processed this way. They're frozen almost as soon as they are picked so all the sweetness is preserved. Adding a little crisp bacon to this soup is a good move too, if you have some, as the smoky saltiness adds another fabulous dimension to the flavour.

50 ml olive oil
1 onion, finely chopped
1 clove garlic, finely chopped
1 litre White Chicken Stock (see page 46)
800 g frozen peas
100 g creme fraiche
¼ cup chopped curly parsley
sea salt and freshly ground black pepper
croutons (see page 94) and chopped
    crisp bacon (optional), to serve

1 Heat the olive oil in a heavy-based saucepan over low heat. Add the onion and garlic and cook, stirring regularly, for 5–6 minutes or until softened but not coloured.

2 Add the stock and bring to the boil. Add the peas and simmer for 10 minutes. Puree the soup in a blender until smooth, then strain through a fine-mesh sieve into a clean pan, pushing down with the bottom of a ladle to extract as much flavour as possible. Stir in the creme fraiche and parsley and season to taste. To serve, top with croutons and bacon, if desired.

Serves 4

Crème de céleri
CREAMY CELERIAC SOUP

Another winner of a winter soup. Celeriac has a really amazing flavour and teams perfectly with potato, which makes the soup very smooth. Creme fraiche is a very Northern French touch and is so much better, I think, than adding ordinary pouring cream. It gives a tanginess to dishes that is more refreshing and 'alive' tasting than regular cream; try using it and I think you will agree.

15 g unsalted butter
1 head celeriac (about 300 g), cut into 3 cm pieces
300 g desiree potatoes, peeled and cut into 3 cm pieces
1 litre White Chicken Stock (see page 46)
100 g creme fraiche
pinch of freshly grated nutmeg
sea salt and freshly ground white pepper

1 Melt the butter in a heavy-based saucepan over low heat. When the butter starts to foam, add the celeriac and potato and stir for 1–2 minutes, then add the stock. Increase the heat to high, bring to the boil, then reduce the heat to low and simmer for 20 minutes or until the vegetables are tender.

2 Puree the soup in a blender until smooth, then add the creme fraiche and season to taste with nutmeg, salt and pepper. Serve.

Serves 4

Soupe à l'oignon
FRENCH ONION SOUP

In France, this is a soup we traditionally eat at around three in the morning after a big wedding or other village event. After everyone has been drinking, dancing and sweating for hours, it's eaten as a reviver. Onions soup is filling and nourishing enough to be an entire meal, but for it to taste truly great, you need to start with a homemade stock.

100 g unsalted butter, chopped
5 onions (about 750 g), halved and thinly sliced
30 g plain flour
1.5 litres White Chicken Stock (see page 46)
sea salt and freshly ground black pepper
chopped curly parsley (optional), to serve
4 slices French baguette or sourdough bread
100 g gruyère (or comté or emmenthal), grated

1 Melt the butter in a large heavy-based casserole over low heat. When it starts to foam, add the onion and cook, stirring regularly, for 30 minutes or until golden. (Keep a close eye on the onion while it cooks as it can catch and burn very quickly.) If the onion starts to stick too much, remove the pan from the heat, cover with a lid and leave to stand for 5 minutes. The steam created will loosen the sticky onion and you can then continue cooking.

2 Sprinkle the flour over the onion and stir for 2 minutes. Add the stock and bring to the boil. Cover and simmer for 15 minutes, stirring regularly. Season to taste with salt and pepper, then remove from the heat. Stir in the parsley (if using).

3 Meanwhile, preheat a griller to high and toast the bread on one side.

4 Place 4 ovenproof bowls on a baking tray and fill each bowl with hot soup, leaving a 2 cm gap at the top. Top each bowl of soup with a slice of bread, toasted-side down, and cover the bread with the grated cheese. Cook under the hot griller for 3–4 minutes or until the cheese is melted and golden. Serve immediately.

Serves 4

Soupe aux lentilles et au bacon
LENTIL AND SPECK SOUP

I normally use the skin from a ham hock in this soup; it flavours it amazingly well. However, you can use speck if that is easier. You can also make a version of this soup by pureeing leftovers from the smoked pork hock and lentils recipe on page 137 with a little cream. Just cook extra of that and turn it into a soup, as the flavours are very similar. Easy!

125 g green puy-style lentils
1 × 100 g piece speck (see page 209), skin on
1½ tablespoons vegetable oil
20 g unsalted butter
2 eschalots, finely chopped
1 clove garlic, finely chopped
1 litre White Chicken Stock (see page 46)
sea salt and freshly ground black pepper
thinly sliced flat-leaf parsley and extra virgin
    olive oil, to serve

1   Soak the lentils in cold water for 4 hours. Drain.

2   Remove the skin from the speck in one piece, taking a thin layer of the meat with it, then reserve the speck for another use.

3   Heat the oil in a heavy-based saucepan over medium heat. Add the butter and when it starts to foam, add the eschalot and garlic. Stir for 4–5 minutes or until translucent. Add the drained lentils and speck skin and stir for 1–2 minutes. Add the stock, then increase the heat to high and bring to the boil. Reduce the heat to low and simmer for 45 minutes or until the lentils are tender.

4   Remove the speck skin and discard. Puree half of the soup in a blender until smooth, then return to the pan, stir to combine and season to taste with salt and pepper.

5   To serve, ladle the soup into bowls, scatter with parsley and drizzle with olive oil.

Serves 4

Potage cressonnière
WATERCRESS SOUP

Watercress makes a soup that I just love eating. That vibrant green colour is so gorgeous and it's really healthy too – like a vitamin tonic in a bowl. As with all of my soups it's dead easy and fast to make, plus you can serve it either hot or cold, depending on the season.

50 g unsalted butter
300 g brushed potatoes such as sebago, peeled and sliced
1 litre White Chicken Stock (see page 46)
2 bunches watercress (about 180 g each), leaves picked,
    washed and coarsely chopped
100 g creme fraiche
sea salt and freshly ground white pepper
watercress sprigs (optional), to serve

1   Melt the butter in a heavy-based saucepan over low heat. When it starts to foam, add the potato and stir for 5 minutes – you don't want it to take on any colour. Add the stock, then increase the heat to medium and bring to the boil. Reduce the heat to low and simmer for 15 minutes or until the potato is tender. Add the watercress and cook for another 2 minutes.

2   Puree the soup in a blender until smooth. Add the creme fraiche and season to taste with salt and pepper.

3   To serve, divide the soup among bowls and top with watercress sprigs, if desired.

Serves 4

SEAFOOD & FISH

Moules marinière
MUSSELS IN WHITE WINE

Although this dish is found all over France these days, it's actually a traditional dish from Brittany and one that I grew up with. The brilliant thing about it is you cook a big potful and just plonk it on the table for everyone to help themselves. Everyone can dig in and once all the mussels are gone there's that fantastic liquor for dunking bread into – mmm. When buying mussels, look for those with firmly shut shells, since opened shells indicate they are well past their prime.

2 kg black mussels, scrubbed and bearded
200 ml dry white wine
2 eschalots, thinly sliced
2 cloves garlic, bruised
2 sprigs thyme
1 bay leaf
5 black peppercorns
200 ml pouring cream
½ cup chopped flat-leaf parsley
freshly ground black pepper
crusty bread, to serve

1   Discard any broken or open mussels. Place the wine, eschalot, garlic, thyme, bay leaf and peppercorns in a large deep frying pan over high heat. Bring to the boil and simmer for 2 minutes. Add 1 kg of the mussels, then cover and shake the pan for 3–4 minutes or just until the shells open. Remove the mussels with tongs or a slotted spoon and transfer to a colander placed over a bowl; you should remove each mussel as soon as the shell opens or they will become tough (some will take longer to cook than others). Repeat with the remaining mussels. Discard any unopened mussels and check each one for any beard that may still be attached to the meat and remove. Place the mussels in a large serving bowl.

2   Strain the mussel cooking liquor though a fine-mesh sieve over a bowl, leaving the last 60 ml in the pan (it will be gritty). Taste the cooking liquor – if it is very salty, dilute with water.

3   Place 250 ml of the mussel cooking liquor in a small saucepan and bring to the boil over medium heat. Add the cream, bring to the boil again, then remove from the heat, stir in the parsley and season to taste with pepper. Pour the sauce over the mussels and serve immediately with crusty bread.

Serves 4

Mouclade
MUSSELS WITH CREAMY SAFFRON SAUCE

This is a more refined dish than the *Moules marinière* on page 66. For a start, the mussels are served in the half-shell. The sauce is thickened with an egg yolk liaison (thickening agent), which is easy to do but adds a level of sophistication. Either present these on individual plates with cutlery, or be less polite and bang down a big, heaving platter and let everyone pick the mussels up with their fingers and slurp them down like oysters. Guess which I do?

2 kg small black mussels, scrubbed and bearded
250 ml dry white wine (or beer or cider)
1 bay leaf
30 g unsalted butter
1 onion, finely chopped
1 clove garlic, finely chopped
pinch of saffron threads
juice of ½ lemon
freshly ground black pepper
2 egg yolks
250 g creme fraiche
chopped flat-leaf parsley, to serve

1　Discard any mussels that are broken or open.

2　Place the wine and bay leaf in a large wide-based frying pan and bring to the boil over high heat. Add 1 kg of the mussels, then cover and shake the pan for 2–3 minutes or until the shells just open. Remove the mussels as soon as the shells open or they will toughen (some will take longer to cook than others). Remove the mussels with a large slotted spoon and place in a colander sitting over a bowl. Repeat with the remaining mussels. Discard any unopened mussels and check each one for any beard that may still be attached to the meat and remove.

3　Place the mussels in a large serving bowl. Strain the mussel cooking liquor through a fine-mesh sieve into a bowl, leaving the last 60 ml behind in the pan (it will be gritty). Taste the cooking liquor – if it is very salty, dilute with water.

4　Meanwhile, melt the butter in a saucepan over low heat. Add the onion and garlic and stir for 6–8 minutes or until soft. Add the saffron and lemon juice and season to taste with pepper. Add the strained cooking liquor, bring to the boil, then remove from the heat.

5　In a separate bowl, combine the egg yolks and creme fraiche. Gradually whisk the egg yolk mixture into the pan, whisking continuously, then return the pan to low heat and whisk until the sauce is just hot.

6　Pour the sauce over the mussels, scatter with parsley and serve immediately.

Serves 6 as an entree or 4 as a main

Homard à l'armoricaine
LOBSTER À L'AMERICAINE

Originally this dish was called Lobster Armorican after Amor, a place in Brittany (and we are famous for our lobsters there!). Somewhere along the line, due to mispronunciation, people started calling it 'American' and the name stuck – but it was invented in Brittany. None of this really matters of course, the dish is just plain delicious regardless of where it was invented.

2 raw lobsters (about 700 g each)
3 litres water
rock salt
500 ml Crab Bisque Sauce (see page 99)
sea salt and freshly ground black pepper (optional)
20 g unsalted butter, softened
flat-leaf parsley sprigs (optional), to serve

1   Place the lobsters in the freezer for 1 hour to put them to sleep before cooking.

2   Place the water and a handful of rock salt in a large saucepan or stockpot and bring to the boil (the lobsters will only draw in the salt that they need). Immerse the lobsters in the boiling water, cook for 3 minutes, then drain and stand until cool. The lobsters should not be cooked all the way through at this point.

3   Twist the bodies from the heads to separate, then scoop the roe out of the heads into a bowl and reserve. Using a large sharp knife or cleaver, coarsely chop the heads and split the tails in half lengthways. Remove the meat from the tails and cut each half into 5 pieces. Clean the tail shells and set aside.

4   Place the bisque in a saucepan, then bring to the boil over medium heat. Reduce the heat to low and simmer for 3 minutes, then check the seasoning and adjust with salt and pepper, if desired.

5   Using a fork, mash the lobster roe with the butter, then whisk the roe mixture into the bisque to thicken it.

6   To serve, transfer the lobster meat to the shells, then pour the bisque sauce over. Garnish with parsley sprigs, if desired.

Serves 4 as an entree

Choucroute de la mer
SEAFOOD CHOUCROUTE

Choucroute is a fairly heavy winter dish from the Alsace region of France that involves loads of sauerkraut and different meats. This simple version is my invention and the idea was to make it more summery by using seafood instead of meat. When I put it on the menu at L'étoile it sold like hotcakes. You can use the sauerkraut that is sold in jars – avoid the tinned stuff as it's not as nice.

200 g small kipfler potatoes, scrubbed
table salt
200 ml dry white wine
2 eschalots, thinly sliced
2 cloves garlic, crushed
2 sprigs thyme
2 bay leaves
10 black peppercorns
500 g black mussels, scrubbed and bearded
400 g clams, soaked in cold water, drained
2 juniper berries

350 g sauerkraut
1 cup finely chopped curly parsley
120 g speck (see page 209), cut into julienne
　　(see page 209)
sea salt and freshly ground black pepper
12 large scallops, roe removed and
　　reserved (optional)
1½ tablespoons olive oil
250 ml Beurre Blanc (see page 96)
finely chopped chervil, to serve

1　Place the potatoes in a saucepan of lightly salted cold water. Bring to the boil over high heat, then simmer for 2 minutes (or if they are thicker than 3 cm, cook for 3–4 minutes). Remove the pan from the heat and leave the potatoes to cool in the water. They should be cooked but still firm. Drain, then cut in half or quarters, depending on the size.

2　Meanwhile, place the wine, eschalot, garlic, thyme, 1 bay leaf and 5 of the peppercorns in a deep, wide-based frying pan over high heat. Bring to the boil and simmer for 2 minutes. Add the mussels, then cover and shake the pan for 2–3 minutes or just until the shells open. Remove the mussels with a slotted spoon as soon as the shells open or they will toughen (some will take longer to cook than others). Place in a colander sitting over a bowl. Add the clams to the pan, then cover and cook for 1–2 minutes or just until the shells open. Transfer the clams to the colander. Discard any unopened mussels and clams. Remove the mussel meat from the shells, removing and discarding any remaining beard.

3　Strain the shellfish cooking liquor through a fine-mesh sieve into a bowl, leaving the last gritty bits behind. Taste the liquor and dilute with water if it is very salty. Place 150 ml of the liquor, the juniper berries and the remaining bay leaf and peppercorns in a small saucepan. Bring to the boil, then add the sauerkraut. Cover and simmer over low heat, stirring occasionally, for 5 minutes. Remove the bay leaf and spices, then stir in the parsley. Meanwhile, place another 150 ml of the shellfish cooking liquor in a wide-based saucepan. Add the potato, mussels, clams, scallop roe, if desired, and speck. Bring to the boil, then reduce the heat to low and simmer for 2–3 minutes or until heated through.

4　Lightly season the scallops. Heat the olive oil in a large heavy-based frying pan over high heat. Cook the scallops for 40 seconds on each side or until just golden, then remove from the pan.

5　To serve, place one-quarter of the sauerkraut in the centre of 4 wide shallow bowls (I use risotto bowls). Using a slotted spoon, top the sauerkraut with mussel and clam mixture and scallops. Drizzle with the warm beurre blanc, scatter with chervil and serve immediately.

Serves 4

Maquereaux à l'escabèche
MACKEREL ESCABECHE

I think mackerel is an underrated fish. It's inexpensive and has a delicious oiliness, rather like tuna. In fact it's related to tuna and I simply don't understand why people don't use it more. Escabeche is a Spanish dish and it's great with a warm potato salad, such as the one on page 12.

8 mackerel fillets (about 85 g each), skin on
sea salt
50 ml olive oil
5 eschalots, thinly sliced lengthways
2 cloves garlic, thinly sliced
1 small carrot, cut into thin rounds
1 sprig thyme
1 fresh bay leaf
250 ml dry white wine
5 black peppercorns
250 ml sherry vinegar (see page 209)
pinch of cayenne pepper or Espelette
    pepper (see page 208)
4 basil leaves
1 lemon, cut into segments (see page 209), then cut
    into small pieces
crusty bread, to serve

1   Season the mackerel on both sides with salt. Heat the olive oil in a large frying pan over low heat and cook 4 of the mackerel fillets, skin-side down, for 20 seconds, then turn and cook for another 10 seconds. Remove from the pan and place, skin-side up, on a wire rack. Repeat with the remaining mackerel.

2   Place the eschalot and garlic in the pan and stir for 3–4 minutes or until soft but not coloured. Add the carrot, thyme, bay leaf and wine. Bring to the boil and simmer until the wine has reduced by half. Add the peppercorns, vinegar, cayenne pepper and basil and simmer for another 5 minutes, then remove from the heat.

3   Place the mackerel, skin-side up, in a deep ceramic dish just large enough to hold it snugly in a single layer. Pour the hot vinegar mixture over the top, cover the dish with foil and leave to stand until cooled to room temperature. Refrigerate for 24 hours.

4   To serve, remove the mackerel escabeche from the refrigerator 30 minutes before serving to allow it to come to room temperature. Scatter with the lemon segments and serve with plenty of crusty bread.

Serves 4 as an entree

Bouillabaisse

BOUILLABAISSE

Here's my take on the Marseilles classic that I adore – it's so moreish! You need to close your eyes when you eat this so you can taste all the different ingredients: the saffron, tomato, herbs and orange and, of course, all the lovely seafood. Use a mix of whatever seafood you want here – lobster, scampi, prawns, clams and mussels all work well. When you serve this dish, don't worry about entree or dessert – you won't need either.

100 ml olive oil
1 large onion, halved and sliced
1 leek, white part only, trimmed, washed and sliced
1 bulb fennel, trimmed and sliced
½ bulb garlic, halved widthways
1 × 400 g tin chopped tomato
1½ tablespoons tomato paste
2½ teaspoons cumin seeds
3 star anise
3 sprigs thyme
1 bay leaf
2 teaspoons black peppercorns
finely grated zest of ½ orange
2 raw blue swimmer crabs, cleaned and cut into 8 pieces (see page 208)

5 kg white fish bones and heads (such as rock cod, latchet, snapper, flathead or whiting), chopped into smaller pieces (to fit your pan)
750 ml dry white wine
2 litres water
24 small kipfler potatoes, scrubbed
1 heaped teaspoon saffron threads
sea salt and cayenne pepper, to taste
1.2 kg mixed white fish fillets (such as rock cod, latchet, snapper, flathead or whiting) and raw shellfish (including lobster, bugs and mussels) halved if large
1 quantity Garlic and Roasted Capsicum Mayonnaise (see page 23)
toasted baguette and thinly sliced flat-leaf parsley, to serve

1   Heat the olive oil in a large heavy-based saucepan or stockpot over medium heat. Add the onion, leek, fennel and garlic and cook, stirring often, for 6–8 minutes or until translucent. Increase the heat to high, then add the tomato, tomato paste, cumin seeds, star anise, thyme, bay leaf, peppercorns and orange zest and stir for another 5–6 minutes or until the mixture has thickened and reduced.

2   Add the crab to the pan and stir for 5 minutes. Add the fish bones and stir for another 5 minutes. Add the wine, then bring to the boil and simmer for 10–12 minutes or until reduced by half. Add the water and bring to the boil again. Reduce the heat to low and simmer for 1 hour. Meanwhile, steam the potatoes over a pan of boiling water for 15 minutes or until tender. When cool enough to handle, peel and set aside.

3   Pour the crab and fish bones into a colander placed over a bowl, then return the stock to the pan. Blend the crab shells in a heavy-duty blender (or use the end of a rolling pin) to crush as much as possible; the more they are crushed, the more flavour will be released. Return the crab shells and fish bones to the pan, combine well, then strain the mixture through a fine mesh sieve into a clean large saucepan, pressing with the bottom of a ladle to remove as much liquid and flavour as possible. Discard the solids.

4   Add the saffron and cayenne, salt and pepper to taste to the pan. (Be generous with the salt, since the soup will take more than you expect, and if it is undersalted, it will not have the rich flavour that bouillabaisse should have.) Place the pan over medium heat and bring to a gentle simmer. Add the fish fillets, shellfish and potatoes and simmer for 5–8 minutes or until the seafood is just cooked through.

5   To serve, divide the seafood and potatoes among large deep bowls. Whisk 60 ml of the mayonnaise into the hot soup, then ladle the soup into the bowls and scatter with parsley. Serve with the remaining mayonnaise and toasted baguette.

Serves 8

Boudin de St-Jacques et bisque de crustacés

SCALLOP BOUDIN WITH CRAB BISQUE SAUCE

This is my signature dish, also fondly known as 'Manu's sausage'. I make it in cooking demonstrations all around Australia and most likely everyone who knows about me also knows about this dish. It's an easy recipe, really; the only truly technical part is in the shaping of the sausage. I find flathead is the right fish for this recipe, but you could use salmon if you want.

250 g flathead fillets, skin removed, pin-boned
90 g egg whites (about 3 egg whites from 55 g eggs)
250 g cleaned scallops, roe removed and discarded, finely chopped
2 tablespoons finely chopped chives
300 ml pouring cream
table salt
500 g baby spinach
50 g cold unsalted butter, chopped
1 quantity Crab Bisque Sauce (see page 99)
sea salt and freshly ground black pepper
ocean trout roe and chervil sprigs, to serve

1   Process the flathead in a food processor until a fine paste forms. Add the egg whites and process until smooth, then transfer the mixture to a large bowl. Fold in the scallop and chives and then, stirring continuously, gradually add the cream and season to taste with salt. (The salt will help 'tighten up' the mixture so it remains firm.) Cover with plastic film and refrigerate for 30 minutes.

2   Lightly dampen a work surface with water and lay out a large piece of plastic film (the water stops the plastic from slipping). Place 100 g of the scallop mixture in a line along the centre of the plastic film, then fold the plastic film over the top and shape the mixture into a sausage about 10 cm long. Roll up and tie a firm knot in the plastic film at each end, then repeat with more plastic film and the remaining mixture to make 8 sausages.

3   Heat a wide-based saucepan of water until it reaches 90°C on a candy thermometer (see page 208) or is just below a simmer. Add the scallop boudin and poach for 10 minutes; the water should not boil or the boudin will split. Gently remove the boudin from the pan and leave to stand for 2–3 minutes. Snip the ends off the plastic film and carefully unwrap the boudin, then pat dry with a clean tea towel.

4   Meanwhile, blanch the spinach in a large saucepan of boiling water for 1 minute, then drain and squeeze out the excess liquid.

5   Just before serving, heat the crab bisque sauce until hot. Whisk in the butter and adjust the seasoning.

6   Divide the crab bisque sauce among 8 shallow soup bowls and place some spinach in a line down the middle. Top with a scallop boudin, a small spoonful of ocean trout roe and a sprig of chervil and serve.

Serves 8 as an entree

Truites aux amandes

RAINBOW TROUT WITH ALMOND BUTTER SAUCE

Another blockbuster classic of French cuisine. If you don't want to deal with whole fish, use the fillets instead (don't forget to pin-bone them). However, don't skimp on the skin if you opt for fillets – the super-crisp texture of the skin and almonds when they've been baked together is what makes this simple dish so fantastic.

2 rainbow trout (about 300 g each), cleaned and scaled
sea salt and freshly ground black pepper
1½ tablespoons vegetable oil
80 g unsalted butter, chopped
60 g flaked almonds, toasted (see page 209)
juice of 1 small lemon
finely chopped flat-leaf parsley, to serve

1 Rinse the trout and pat dry with paper towel. Season to taste with salt and pepper on both sides and inside the cavity.

2 Heat the oil and 20 g of the butter in a large heavy-based frying pan or saute pan over medium heat. When the butter starts to foam, add the fish and cook for 3 minutes on each side or until golden but still a little pink on the inside. If the butter starts to burn, reduce the heat a little. Place the fish on plates and return the pan to the heat.

3 Add the remaining butter and cook over low heat. When the butter starts to foam, add the almonds, lemon juice and parsley. Check the seasoning, then pour the sauce over the fish (or return the fish to the pan, see opposite) and serve immediately.

Serves 2 as a main

Saumon à l'oseille
SALMON WITH SORREL BUTTER SAUCE

In France salmon and sorrel are regarded as a classic combination – sorrel has a gorgeous, fresh citrusy flavour that is an excellent counterbalance to the oiliness of salmon. This is a stylish dish but extremely quick to make, as everything cooks at the last minute; I like serving it with my Zucchini Flans (see page 145).

4 × 200 g salmon fillets, skin-on and pin-boned
50 ml olive oil
Zucchini Flans (optional, see page 145), to serve

Sorrel butter
2 eschalots, finely chopped
150 ml dry white wine
1½ tablespoons vermouth (such as Noily Pratt or
    White Martini, see page 209)
100 ml Fish Stock (see page 47)
150 ml pouring cream or creme fraiche
90 g cold unsalted butter, chopped
1 bunch sorrel, stalks removed and leaves shredded
sea salt and freshly ground black pepper
lemon juice, to taste

1   Remove the salmon from the refrigerator and allow it to come to room temperature.

2   Meanwhile, to make the sorrel butter, place the eschalot, wine, vermouth and stock in a saucepan and bring to the boil over medium heat. Simmer for 10–12 minutes or until reduced by half, then add the cream and simmer for 6–8 minutes or until reduced by half again. Reduce the heat to low, then whisk in the butter, one piece at a time, until the sauce is thick and emulsified. Add the sorrel, stir until just wilted, then remove from the heat and season to taste with salt, pepper and a dash of lemon juice.

3   Heat the olive oil in a large frying pan over medium heat. Cook the salmon, skin-side down first, for 4 minutes or until the skin is golden and crisp; do not move the fish during this time or the skin may stick to the pan and tear. Reduce the heat to low, turn the fish and cook for another 2–3 minutes or until cooked but still pink in the middle. Remove from the pan and leave to stand for 5 minutes.

4   To serve, divide the salmon among serving plates, then top with the sorrel butter sauce and a grind of black pepper. Serve with zucchini flans alongside, if desired.

Serves 4 as a main

Duarade en croûte de sel
SALT-CRUST BAKED SNAPPER

This is the easiest way to cook fish, ever. The salt crust creates a sort of mini-oven around the fish and keeps all the moisture trapped inside, resulting in the juiciest fish you'll ever taste. The most important thing here is to leave the scales on the fish: otherwise, the crust will stick to the skin and over-season the fish. And remember, the salt crust is just for cooking, not eating!

4 sprigs thyme
4 small fresh bay leaves
1 small lemon, thinly sliced
1 × 2 kg snapper, cleaned, scales intact (ask
    your fishmonger to do this if you prefer)
freshly ground black pepper
1.5 kg table salt
6 egg whites

1 Preheat the oven to 200°C.

2 Place the thyme, bay leaves and lemon slices inside the cavity of the fish and season the cavity with pepper.

3 Place the salt and egg whites in a large bowl and whisk to combine well. Spread a 1 cm thick layer of the salt mixture over a large baking tray, keeping it in the shape of the snapper as much as possible. Place the fish on top of the salt mixture, then spread the remaining salt mixture over the top and sides to cover it completely. Bake the snapper for 45 minutes, then remove from the oven. The salt crust should have become a hard golden shell.

4 To serve, crack the salt crust at the table in front of your guests. (Do not eat the salt shell – it is only used for cooking.)

Serves 4 as a main

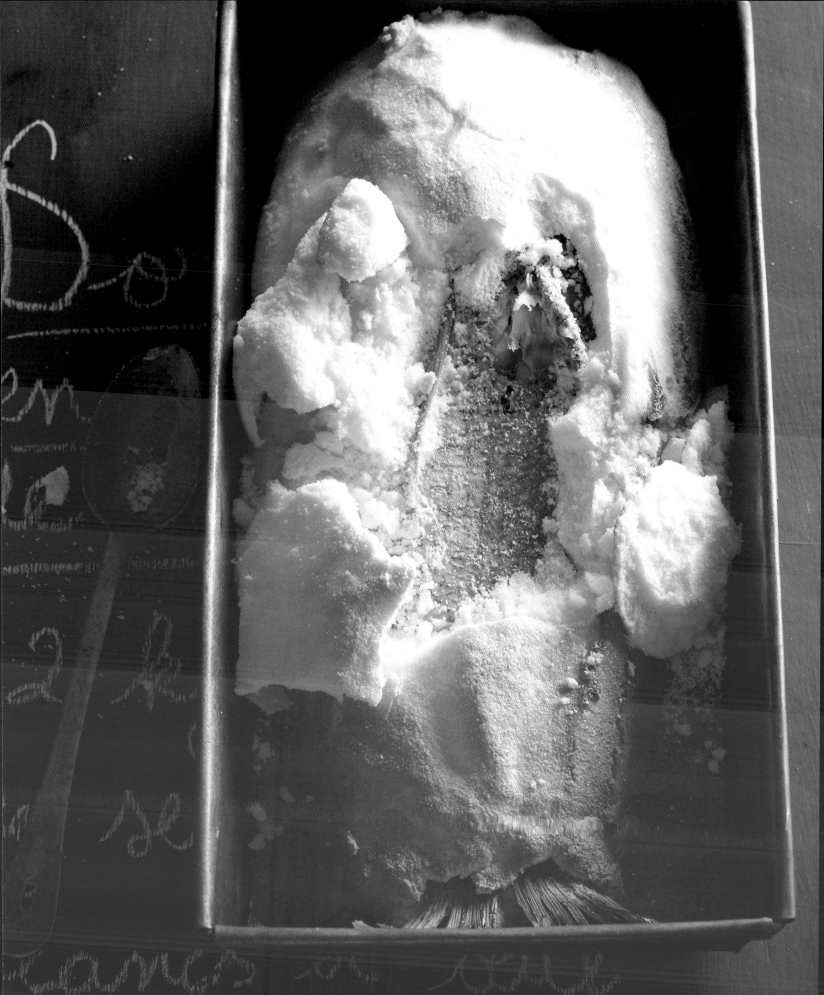

Carbonara de truite de mer fumée

SMOKED OCEAN TROUT CARBONARA

This is one of Mum's recipes; the smoked ocean trout takes the place of the more usual bacon. Make sure, though, that you use ocean trout from a whole, cold-smoked side – please don't use pre-sliced ocean trout as it will quickly overcook to mush and fall apart. You want the fish to still be opaque and only just warmed through.

400 g fresh tagliatelle
table salt
2 teaspoons extra virgin olive oil
1 × 200 g piece smoked ocean trout, cut into
    3 cm × 1 cm strips (lardons, see page 209)
100 ml Fish Stock (see page 47)
2–3 tablespoons lemon juice
150 g sour cream
sea salt and freshly ground black pepper
1 egg yolk
finely chopped chives, to serve

1   Cook the pasta in a large saucepan of lightly salted boiling water for 2–3 minutes, then drain.

2   Meanwhile, heat the olive oil in a large frying pan over low heat. Add the ocean trout and stir for 1 minute, then add the stock, lemon juice and sour cream. Season to taste with salt and pepper and bring to a simmer.

3   Add the drained pasta to the pan and toss to coat with the sauce. Add the egg yolk and chives, check the seasoning and serve immediately.

Serves 4

Sole meunière

FLOUNDER WITH LEMON BUTTER SAUCE

I just LOVE flounder; it's one of my favourite Australian fish. I particularly love how the skin goes so crisp. It's an excellent fish for kids, too, because there aren't any bones through the flesh so it's easy for them to deal with. You don't need to 'do' anything to flounder, either – it begs to be cooked whole and served with a simple, tasty butter. Heaven on a plate!

2 × 300 g flounder
sea salt and freshly ground black pepper
1½ tablespoons vegetable oil
150 g unsalted butter, chopped
juice of ½ lemon
¼ cup chopped curly parsley
1 lemon, halved (optional), to serve

1   Preheat the oven to 180°C.

2   Using a long, sharp, flexible knife, carefully remove the skin from one side of the fish and season with salt and pepper on both sides.

3   Heat the oil and 20 g of the butter in a large ovenproof frying pan over medium–high heat. When the butter starts to foam, cook the fish skin-side down for 4–5 minutes or until golden. Turn the fish over, then transfer to the oven to cook for another 5 minutes or until just cooked through.

4   To serve, transfer the fish to a serving plate. Place the pan over high heat, then add the remaining butter and swirl the pan until it begins to foam. Add a good squeeze of lemon juice and the parsley to the sauce and check the seasoning, then spoon over the fish. Serve with the lemon, if desired.

Serves 2 as a main

Whiting en papillote et légumes parfumés à l'estragon
PAPILLOTE OF WHITING AND TARRAGON-SCENTED VEGETABLES

The great thing about this dish is that it's easy to know when to take it out of the oven – when the foil parcel has puffed up your fish is cooked. The other advantage is that all the delicious flavours are locked in until you open up the parcel at the table.

1 tablespoon olive oil, plus extra for drizzling
2 carrots, cut into julienne (see page 209)
2 leeks, cut into julienne (see page 209)
¼ cup french tarragon, thinly sliced
sea salt and freshly ground black pepper
8 King George whiting fillets, skin-on and pin-boned
100 g unsalted butter, chopped
1 lemon, thinly sliced
125 ml dry white wine

1   Heat the olive oil in a large frying pan over medium heat. Add the carrot and leek and stir for 6–8 minutes or until just soft. Stir in most of the tarragon and season to taste with salt and pepper. Remove from the heat and set aside to cool.

2   Preheat the oven to 180°C.

3   Place four 50 cm long pieces of heavy-duty foil, shiny-side down, on a work surface and cover each with a piece of baking paper. Drizzle a little olive oil on one side of each piece of the baking paper-lined foil, then top with carrot and leek mixture. Place 2 fish fillets, skin side down, over the carrot and leek mixture and top each fillet with 25 g butter and a few slices of lemon. Season to taste with salt and pepper and scatter with the remaining tarragon. Fold over the other side of foil to cover, then fold in two of the sides to seal the parcel well – as if you are making an envelope. Pour one quarter of the wine into each parcel, then fold over the remaining side to fully enclose the fish and vegetables.

4   Transfer the parcels to a baking tray and bake for 15 minutes or until the bags have inflated and the fish is cooked through. Serve.

Serves 4 as a main

Brandade de morue
BRANDADE

You can buy bacalau (dried salt cod) for this recipe or do what I do – I keep all my fish trimmings and pack them in rock salt with some fresh thyme and bay leaves, leave them in the fridge for twenty-four hours to cure, then rinse the fish and use it for this recipe. You don't have to use trimmings for salting; you can use fillets if you like. Whatever type of salted fish you choose, your brandade will still be delicious.

500 g dried salt cod fillets, soaked in cold water for
    24 hours, water changed 6 times
1 sprig thyme
1 bay leaf
1 litre milk
400 g brushed potatoes such as sebago, peeled and halved
5 cloves garlic, peeled
250 ml pouring cream
100 ml olive oil, plus extra for drizzling
2 tablespoons finely chopped dill
sea salt and freshly ground white pepper
pinch of cayenne pepper
lemon juice, to taste
100 g coarse breadcrumbs, made from day-old bread

1 Drain the salt cod, then cut into 5 cm pieces. Place the salt cod, thyme, bay leaf and 500 ml of the milk in a saucepan. Bring to the boil over medium heat, then reduce the heat to low and simmer for 10 minutes. Remove the pan from the heat, drain the salt cod and discard the milk and herbs. When the salt cod is cool enough to handle, remove and discard the skin and bones and set the flesh aside.

2 Meanwhile, place the potato in a saucepan with the remaining milk, whole garlic cloves and cream. Bring to the boil over medium heat, then reduce the heat to low and simmer for 20 minutes or until the potato is tender. Drain the potato and garlic in a colander placed over a bowl and reserve the milk mixture.

3 Preheat the oven to 200°C.

4 Using an electric mixer fitted with a paddle attachment, combine the potato, garlic and fish. With the motor running, gradually add the olive oil, then add all but 125 ml of the reserved milk mixture and beat until smooth. If the mixture is still a little thick, then add a little more of the reserved milk until you achieve your desired consistency. Add the dill and season to taste with salt, pepper, cayenne pepper and lemon juice.

5 Spoon the mixture into a 1.25 litre capacity gratin dish. Sprinkle the breadcrumbs over the top, drizzle with a little extra olive oil and bake for 10–15 minutes or until golden.

6 Serve at room temperature.

Serves 6–8 as an entree

Aile de raie aux câpres
SKATE WITH CAPER BUTTER SAUCE

If you can get your hands on skate then give this dish a go. It is a wonderful fish and not used nearly enough. Skate cooked in this way is another of my all-time favourite dishes. The skate needs to be skinned, which can be a little tricky, so ask your fishmonger nicely to do this for you, if you prefer. One thing to remember about skate is that it is highly perishable and doesn't keep well.

4 × 250 g pieces skate wing, skin removed
sea salt and freshly ground black pepper
120 g unsalted butter, chopped
juice of 1 lemon
1 cup chopped curly parsley
40 g small salted capers, rinsed very well and
    patted dry with paper towel

Court-bouillon
1 small onion, thinly sliced
1 small carrot, thinly sliced
2 teaspoons fennel seeds
50 ml white-wine vinegar
1½ teaspoons black peppercorns
2 teaspoons coarse sea salt
3 litres water

1   Rinse the skate wings and pat dry with paper towel.

2   To make the court-bouillon, place the onion, carrot, fennel seeds, vinegar, peppercorns, salt and water in a large saucepan and bring to the boil over medium heat. Remove from the heat, then leave to stand for 10 minutes.

3   Add the skate wings to the court-bouillon and place over very low heat for 10 minutes; the liquid should not boil. Carefully remove the skate, pat dry with paper towel, then season to taste with salt and pepper.

4   Place 30 g of the butter in a large frying pan over medium heat. When the butter starts to foam but is not brown, add the skate and cook for 3–4 minutes or until golden on both sides. Transfer the skate to serving plates, then add the remaining butter to the pan over low heat. When the butter starts to foam, add the lemon juice, parsley and capers and swirl the pan until all the ingredients are well combined. Pour the caper butter sauce over the skate and serve immediately.

Serves 4 as a main

Kingfish à la grenobloise
PAN-ROASTED KINGFISH WITH LEMON, CAPER AND CROUTON BUTTER SAUCE

Here's a classic French combination given an Aussie twist by using kingfish. It makes a really quick but classy main course for lunch or dinner. The delicious hiramasa (farmed kingfish from South Australia) we now have is great because it means there is a year-round supply of an otherwise seasonal fish and that the kingfish are always of a consistent size.

50 ml olive oil
4 × 200 g kingfish fillets, skin on
sea salt and freshly ground black pepper
100 g unsalted butter, chopped
1 lemon, cut into segments (see page 209)
40 g salted baby capers, rinsed well
⅓ cup chopped flat-leaf parsley
mixed leaf salad, to serve

Croutons
2 tablespoons olive oil
20 g unsalted butter
4 slices good-quality white bread, crusts
    removed, cut into 5 mm cubes

1 Preheat the oven to 180°C.

2 To make the croutons, heat the olive oil and butter in a large ovenproof frying pan over medium heat. Add the bread and shake the pan for 5–6 minutes or until golden and crisp. Drain on paper towel and wipe the pan clean.

3 Add the olive oil to the pan and place over medium heat. Season the fish with salt and pepper, then cook, skin-side down, for 4–5 minutes or until golden. Turn the fish over, then transfer the pan to the oven and cook the fish for 5 minutes or until it is just cooked through. Remove from the pan and place on serving plates.

4 Pour off any fat from the pan and return to low heat. Add the butter, and as soon as it starts to foam, add the lemon segments, capers, croutons and parsley and toss to combine well.

5 Pour the sauce over the fish fillets and serve immediately with a mixed leaf salad.

Serves 4 as a main

Sauce de beurre blanc
BEURRE BLANC

3 eschalots, finely chopped
60 ml dry white wine
1½ tablespoons white-wine vinegar
1½ tablespoons pouring cream
250 g unsalted butter, slightly softened and chopped
lemon juice, to taste
sea salt and freshly ground white pepper

Place the eschalot, wine and vinegar in a small saucepan and simmer over low heat for 4–5 minutes or until reduced to about 1 tablespoon. Whisk in the cream, then reduce the heat to as low as possible.

Whisking continuously, add the butter one piece at a time until the sauce is creamy and emulsified. Be careful not to boil the mixture at all or the sauce will split.

Strain the sauce through a fine-mesh sieve into a bowl, discard the solids, then season with lemon juice, salt and pepper.

Serve immediately, or if you wish, pour into a small bowl, cover the surface with a round of baking paper and keep in a warm but not too hot spot near the stove for 1 hour.

Make about 250 ml

VARIATION: BEURRE ROUGE

For a simple variation of beurre blanc, substitute the white wine with red wine and the white-wine vinegar with red-wine vinegar. This version pairs beautifully with steak or perhaps brioche stuffed with bone marrow.

Sauce béarnaise
BEARNAISE SAUCE

250 g unsalted butter, chopped
3 eschalots, finely chopped
60 ml dry white wine
1½ tablespoons white-wine vinegar
1 teaspoon dried tarragon
1 teaspoon lightly crushed black peppercorns
4 egg yolks
sea salt
2 teaspoons chopped french tarragon
2 teaspoons chopped chervil
lemon juice, to taste
freshly ground white pepper

Melt the butter in a small saucepan over low heat, then simmer until the milk solids separate and fall to the bottom of the pan; be careful not to burn the butter. Strain off the clear butter and discard the milk solids. This is known as clarified butter.

Meanwhile, place the eschalot, wine, vinegar, dried tarragon and peppercorns in a small saucepan and simmer over low heat for 4–5 minutes or until reduced to 1½ tablespoons. Strain through a fine-mesh sieve into a bowl, discard the solids and set the reduction aside to cool.

Half-fill a saucepan with water and bring to a very gentle simmer over low heat. Combine the egg yolks, wine reduction and a pinch of salt in a large heatproof bowl that fits snugly over the saucepan – the bottom of the bowl should not touch the water. Whisk for 8–10 minutes or until the mixture leaves a trail and is thick and creamy. Be careful not to overheat the egg mixture or it will scramble.

Pour the water out of the saucepan, then place the bowl back over the saucepan, off the heat – this helps stabilise the bowl while you whisk in the clarified butter. Whisk a thin stream of the warm clarified butter into the egg mixture until thick and emulsified, whisking continuously. Stir in the fresh tarragon and chervil and season to taste with lemon juice, salt and pepper.

Serve immediately, or if you wish, pour into a small bowl, cover the surface with a round of baking paper and keep in a warm but not too hot spot near the stove for 1 hour.

Makes about 375 ml

Sauce Choron
TOMATO BEARNAISE

250 g unsalted butter, chopped
3 eschalots, finely chopped
60 ml dry white wine
1½ tablespoons white-wine vinegar
1 teaspoon dried tarragon
1 teaspoon lightly crushed black peppercorns
4 egg yolks
sea salt
2 tomatoes, peeled, seeded (see page 209) and
    finely chopped
1 teaspoon tomato paste
lemon juice, to taste
freshly ground white pepper

Melt the butter in a small saucepan over low heat, then simmer until the milk solids separate and fall to the bottom of the pan; be careful not to burn the butter. Strain off the clear butter and discard the milk solids. This is known as clarified butter.

Meanwhile, place the eschalot, wine, vinegar, tarragon and peppercorns in a small saucepan and simmer over low heat until reduced to 1½ tablespoons. Strain through a fine-mesh sieve over a bowl, discard the solids and cool the reduction.

Half-fill a saucepan with water and bring to a very gentle simmer. Combine the egg yolks, wine reduction and a pinch of salt in a large heatproof bowl that fits snugly over the saucepan; the bottom of the bowl should not touch the water. Whisk over low heat for 8–10 minutes or until the mixture leaves a trail and is thick and creamy. Be careful not to overheat the egg mixture or it will scramble.

Pour the water out of the saucepan, then place the bowl back over the saucepan, off the heat – this helps to stabilise the bowl while you whisk in the clarified butter. Whisk a thin stream of the warm clarified butter into the egg mixture until thick and emulsified, whisking continuously. Stir in the chopped tomato and tomato paste and season to taste with lemon juice, salt and pepper.

Serve immediately, or if you wish, pour into a small bowl, cover the surface with a round of baking paper and keep in a warm but not too hot spot near the stove for 1 hour.

Makes about 375 ml

Sauce hollandaise
HOLLANDAISE SAUCE

250 g unsalted butter, chopped
4 egg yolks
60 ml dry white wine
sea salt
juice of ½ lemon
freshly ground white pepper

Melt the butter in a small saucepan over low heat, then simmer until the milk solids separate and fall to the bottom of the pan; be careful not to burn the butter. Strain off the clear butter and discard the milk solids. This is known as clarified butter.

Half-fill a saucepan with water and bring to a very gentle simmer. Combine the egg yolks, wine and a pinch of salt in a large heatproof bowl which fits snugly over the saucepan; the bottom of the bowl should not touch the water. Be careful not to overheat the egg mixture or it will scramble. Whisk for 8–10 minutes or until the mixture leaves a trail and is thick and creamy.

Pour the water out of the saucepan, then place the bowl back over the saucepan, off the heat – this helps to stabilise the bowl while you whisk in the clarified butter. Whisk a thin stream of the warm clarified butter into the egg mixture until thick and emulsified, whisking continuously. Whisk in the lemon juice and season to taste with salt and pepper.

Serve immediately, or if you wish, pour into a small bowl, cover the surface with a round of baking paper and keep in a warm but not too hot spot near the stove for 1 hour.

Makes about 430 ml

Sauce béchamel
BECHAMEL SAUCE

1 litre milk
sea salt and freshly ground white pepper
freshly grated nutmeg
60 g unsalted butter, chopped
60 g plain flour

Place the milk in a saucepan and season to taste with salt, pepper and nutmeg. Bring to the boil, then remove from the heat.

Melt the butter in a saucepan over low heat. When the butter starts to foam, add the flour and stir for 2–3 minutes or until the mixture becomes sand-coloured (this is called a roux). Remove from the heat and leave to cool for 5 minutes.

With the pan still off the heat and whisking continuously, gradually add the hot milk to the roux, then place the pan over medium heat. Whisk until the mixture boils and thickens, then reduce the heat to low. Simmer for 20 minutes, whisking frequently to prevent the bechamel from catching. Strain through a fine-mesh sieve into a bowl and season to taste with salt and pepper. If you need to cool the bechamel for use later, cover the surface with a piece of plastic film to prevent a skin forming.

Makes about 850 ml

Sauce Bordelaise
RICH RED-WINE SAUCE

80 g unsalted butter, chopped
8 eschalots (about 200 g), finely chopped
400 g field mushrooms, sliced
3 sprigs thyme
1 bay leaf
3 sprigs french tarragon
1 star anise
3 juniper berries
3 teaspoons black peppercorns, lightly cracked
3 cloves garlic, bruised
2 wide strips orange rind, white pith removed
1 tomato, chopped
1.5 litres red wine
50 ml port
1½ tablespoons balsamic vinegar
1.5 litres Brown Veal Stock (see page 47)
sea salt and freshly ground black pepper

Melt 30 g of the butter in a large heavy-based saucepan over medium heat. When the butter starts to foam, add the eschalot and stir for 2–3 minutes or until soft. Increase the heat to high, then add the mushrooms, thyme, bay leaf, tarragon, star anise, juniper berries, peppercorns, garlic and orange rind and stir for 6–8 minutes or until the mushrooms are golden. Reduce the heat to low, then add the tomato and stir for another 5 minutes.

Add the wine, port and vinegar to the pan and bring to the boil. Simmer for 15 minutes or until reduced by one-third, then add the stock and simmer again for 30 minutes or until reduced by half.

Strain the sauce through a fine-mesh sieve into a clean pan and discard the solids. Simmer the sauce over medium heat for 6–8 minutes or until reduced to a light sauce consistency; do not reduce too much or the flavour will be too intense. Reduce the heat to low and whisk in the remaining 50 g butter, then season to taste with salt and pepper.

Serves 12

TIPS AND TRICKS

If freezing half of the sauce for later use, only add half the butter (25 g) to the remainder.

Bisque de crabe
CRAB BISQUE SAUCE

1 kg raw blue swimmer crabs (about 4)
50 ml olive oil
1 small onion, chopped
1 bulb baby fennel, trimmed and chopped
2 stalks celery, chopped
4 eschalots, chopped
8 cloves garlic, chopped
5 cm knob ginger, chopped
5 roma (plum) tomatoes, chopped
50 ml brandy
250 ml dry white wine
1 tablespoon tomato paste
2 star anise
5 black peppercorns
¼ teaspoon coriander seeds
¼ teaspoon fennel seeds
3 sprigs thyme
1 bay leaf
2 litres cold water
250 ml pouring cream
50 g cold unsalted butter, chopped
sea salt and freshly ground black pepper

Working with one crab at a time, hold a crab upside down, then lift the tail flaps ('apron') and insert a small knife under the top shell. Twist the knife to loosen and pull off the top shell, then remove and discard the grey gills ('dead man's fingers'). Leave the coral ('mustard') as it holds a lot of flavour. Using a kitchen cleaver or large sharp knife, cut each crab body into 8 pieces and tap the large claws firmly to break open the shell. Set aside.

Heat the olive oil in a large heavy-based saucepan or stockpot over high heat. Place the crab pieces in the pan and cook, stirring often, for 6–8 minutes or until the shells change colour. Add the onion, fennel, celery, eschalot, garlic and ginger and stir for 8–10 minutes or until lightly coloured. Add the tomato and brandy and simmer until reduced by half. Pour in the wine and simmer for 5–6 minutes or until reduced by half again, then add the tomato paste, star anise, peppercorns, coriander seeds, fennel seeds, thyme, bay leaf and water and bring to the boil. Reduce the heat to low and simmer, without skimming, for 40 minutes.

Strain the mixture through a colander sitting over a large bowl, then return the solids to the pan and reserve the stock. Using a heavy-duty blender (or the end of a rolling pin), crush the shells as much as possible – the more you crush them, the more flavour will be released. Return the stock and crushed shells to the pan, combine well, then strain the mixture through a fine-mesh sieve into a large bowl, pressing with the bottom of a ladle to remove as much liquid and flavour as possible. Discard the solids.

Transfer 1 litre of the stock to a clean saucepan. Add the cream and simmer over low heat for 15–20 minutes or until the bisque has reduced enough to coat the back of a wooden spoon. Whisk the butter into the hot bisque sauce, then season with salt and pepper.

Makes about 1 litre

Meat, Poultry and Game

Joues de boeuf bourguignon
BEEF CHEEK BOURGUIGNON

I love to use beef cheek in this dish. It's such a gorgeous, rich cut that is just perfect for braising. This is one recipe that needs a good-quality red wine – a cheap 'cooking' wine changes the flavour completely and the dish truly suffers, so it's worth buying a great red wine. Just make sure you buy an extra bottle to drink with it.

1 onion, coarsely chopped
3 eschalots, coarsely chopped
2 carrots, coarsely chopped
2 cloves garlic, bruised
1 litre red wine (burgundy or pinot noir)
1 sprig thyme
1 bay leaf
1 teaspoon black peppercorns
1.5 kg beef cheeks, trimmed and connective
    tissue removed, cut into halves
1½ tablespoons vegetable oil
60 g unsalted butter, chopped
sea salt

20 g plain flour
flat-leaf parsley leaves (optional), to serve

Garnish
8 pearl onions, peeled, root ends intact
large pinch of caster sugar
30 g unsalted butter
sea salt and freshly ground black pepper
1 × 200 g piece speck (see page 209), cut into
    3 cm × 1 cm strips (lardons, see page 209)
50 ml vegetable oil
400 g button mushrooms, wiped clean

1   Place the onion, eschalot, carrot, garlic, red wine, thyme, bay leaf and peppercorns in a large bowl. Add the beef and combine well. Cover with plastic film and refrigerate overnight.

2   Remove the meat from the marinade and pat dry well with paper towel. Set aside. Strain the marinade through a fine-mesh sieve into a large bowl and set aside; reserve the vegetables and herbs.

3   Heat the oil and butter in a large enamelled cast-iron casserole over medium–high heat. When the butter begins to foam, cook the meat in batches, seasoning it with salt as you go, for 8–10 minutes or until golden all over. Remove from the pan, reduce the heat to low, then add the reserved vegetables and herbs and stir for 6–8 minutes or until light golden. Return the meat to the pan, sprinkle over the flour and stir over low heat for 1 minute. Add the reserved marinade, scraping the pan to remove any cooked-on bits, and bring to the boil. Simmer, covered, for 2–3 hours or until the beef is tender, regularly skimming the surface of any impurities. (The cooking time will vary depending on the quality of the meat.)

4   Meanwhile, to make the garnish, place the onions, sugar, butter and a pinch of salt and pepper in a small saucepan. Add enough water to come halfway up the side of the onions, then cover and cook over medium heat for 10 minutes. Cook, uncovered, for another 5 minutes or until all the water has evaporated and the onions are tender and lightly coloured. Set aside. Heat a large frying pan over medium heat. Add the speck and cook for 6–7 minutes or until golden, then remove from the pan and set aside. Add the oil and, when hot, add the mushrooms and season to taste with salt and pepper. Toss for 5–6 minutes or until golden and tender.

5   Drain the meat and vegetables in a colander placed over a large bowl, then strain the sauce through a fine-mesh sieve into a large saucepan. Use a ladle to remove the fat from the surface of the sauce. Discard the vegetables in the colander. Add the meat, glazed onions, mushrooms and speck to the sauce. Simmer over low heat for 15 minutes or until the sauce has thickened and reduced. Check the seasoning, add the flat-leaf parsley, if desired, and serve.

Serves 4 as a main

Comment cuire un steak
HOW TO PAN-FRY STEAK

You might wonder why I'd bother giving a detailed recipe for cooking steak. It's because the simplest things can be the hardest to get right and people often ask me how I can tell when a steak is cooked. Although the process isn't difficult, you do need to concentrate on what you are doing and follow a few rules. However, once you've mastered the art you'll be cooking steak like a pro! Don't use olive oil for frying your steak as its smoking point is lower than that of other vegetable oils. For example, grapeseed oil has a smoking point of 250°C, while olive oil starts to smoke at 190°C. Using an oil with a higher smoking point means that the pan can be much hotter before the oil starts to smoke.

4 × 250 g steaks (such as rib-eye, sirloin or rump)
2 tablespoons vegetable oil
fleur de sel (see page 208)
freshly ground black pepper
30 g unsalted butter

1   Remove the steaks from the refrigerator 30 minutes before cooking. (Having the meat at room temperature before you cook means it cooks more evenly than meat that is very cold. It also means that if you like your steak rare or blue (see below), the centre won't be cold after cooking.)

2   Heat the oil in a large heavy-based frying pan over high heat. Season the steaks well on both sides with salt and pepper. When the oil is hot, reduce the heat to low and add the butter. When the butter starts to foam, add the steaks. (The butter is a good indicator of whether the temperature is correct: if the butter doesn't foam when it is added to the hot oil, it means the pan isn't hot enough. If it starts burning, it's too hot. The perfect temperature is around 170–180°C, which is when the butter turns nut-brown.)

3   Although the following times will vary depending on the thickness of your steak (and pan), as a rough guide cooking times are:

   - For blue: 2 minutes on each side
   - For rare: 3–4 minutes on each side
   - For medium–rare: 4–5 minutes on each side
   - For medium: 5–6 minutes on each side
   - For medium–well and well done: over 6 minutes on each side

4   During cooking, rotate the steaks from time to time and spoon the cooking fat over them. Remove the steaks from the pan and leave to rest for 5 minutes on a wire rack placed over a baking tray near the stove. (The resting allows the meat to 'relax' and release its juices. It is better to serve a warm, well-rested steak than a piping hot one straight from the pan.) Pour any resting juices over the top of the steaks, then serve.

Serves 4 as a main

Steak au Roquefort
STEAK WITH ROQUEFORT SAUCE

My dad had this on his restaurant menu and I was completely addicted to it. I didn't eat steak with Roquefort sauce for years and years and then one day I suddenly got the idea to put it on my restaurant menu and see what happened. I thought people might think it a bit old-fashioned, but they loved it! You must use Roquefort, though – don't even think of using any other blue cheese as it just won't taste the same.

4 × 250 g beef fillet or rump steaks
sea salt and freshly ground black pepper
1½ tablespoons vegetable oil
20 g unsalted butter
3 eschalots, finely chopped
1 clove garlic, finely chopped
150 ml dry white wine
150 ml White Chicken Stock (see page 46)
200 g Roquefort cheese, crumbled
100 ml pouring cream

1   Remove the steaks from the refrigerator 30 minutes before cooking.

2   Season the steaks with salt and pepper.

3   Heat the oil and butter in a large heavy-based frying pan over medium heat. When the butter starts to foam, add the steaks and cook for 3 minutes on each side or until golden and cooked to your liking. Remove the steaks from the pan and leave to rest for 5 minutes.

4   Add the eschalot and garlic to the pan and stir over low–medium heat for 2–3 minutes or until golden. Add the wine and carefully tilt the pan towards the flame to ignite the alcohol (or use a lighter if necessary). When the flames have subsided, add the stock and simmer until reduced by half. Reduce the heat to low, then whisk in the cheese. Add the cream and simmer until slightly thickened and reduced to a sauce consistency. Adjust the seasoning, then return the steaks and any resting juices to the pan, turn to coat and serve.

Serves 4 as a main

Steak au poivre

STEAK WITH PEPPERCORN SAUCE

Using homemade stock makes an unbelievable difference to the end result here. And don't skimp on the brandy as it gives the sauce that certain *je ne sais quoi*. But believe me, it's best to use no port at all than a cheapie – bad port will make the dish taste sweet and nasty.

4 × 250 g beef fillet or rump steaks
50 g black peppercorns, coarsely cracked
1½ tablespoons vegetable oil
60 g unsalted butter, chopped
4 eschalots, finely chopped
1 clove garlic, finely chopped
80 ml brandy
80 ml port
150 ml Brown Veal Stock (see page 47) or beef stock
100 g creme fraiche
sea salt

1 Remove the steaks from the refrigerator 30 minutes before cooking.

2 Roll the steaks in the cracked pepper.

3 Heat the oil and butter in a large heavy-based frying pan over medium–high heat. When the butter starts to foam, add the steaks and cook for 3 minutes on each side or until a golden crust forms and the steaks are cooked to your liking. Remove the steaks from the pan and leave to rest in a warm place for 5 minutes.

4 Meanwhile, return the pan to low heat. Add the eschalot and garlic and stir for 1 minute or until light golden. Add the brandy and carefully tilt the pan towards the flame to ignite the alcohol (or use a lighter). When the flames have subsided, add the port and simmer until reduced by half. Add the stock and simmer until reduced by half again. Add the creme fraiche and simmer until reduced to the consistency of pouring cream. Season to taste with salt, then return the steaks and any resting juices to the pan. Turn to coat and simmer for 30 seconds, then serve.

Serves 4 as a main

Bavette à l'échalote
STEAK WITH ESCHALOTS

Bavette is the name of the most popular beef cut for steak in France. It's chewier than other steaks, but the flavour is just incredible. It took me months to convince diners in my restaurant that this is better than eye fillet. It's real steak with real flavour!

4 × 250 g pieces beef skirt steak
70 g unsalted butter, chopped
10 eschalots, thinly sliced
50 ml dry white wine
50 ml Brown Veal Stock (see page 47) or beef stock
⅓ cup flat-leaf parsley leaves
sea salt and freshly ground black pepper
50 ml vegetable oil

1   Remove the steaks from the refrigerator 30 minutes before cooking.

2   Melt 50 g of the butter in a small heavy-based saucepan over medium heat. Add the eschalot and cook for 4–5 minutes or until soft. If the butter looks like it is browning, reduce the heat to low. Add the wine and stock, then reduce the heat to low and simmer for 5–6 minutes or until the mixture is slightly thickened and reduced. Add the parsley, then remove from the heat and keep warm.

3   Season the steaks with salt and pepper. Heat the oil in a large frying pan over medium–high heat. Cook the steaks for 1–2 minutes on each side or until just until golden, then reduce the heat to low and add the remaining butter. Cook the steaks for another 2 minutes, then remove from the pan and place on a wire rack placed over a baking tray to rest for 4 minutes.

4   Using a large sharp knife, slice the beef against the grain at a 90-degree angle. Divide among serving plates, then spoon the eschalot sauce over and serve.

Serves 4 as a main

Steak haché à cheval

PAN-FRIED BEEF RISSOLE WITH AN EGG SUNNY-SIDE UP

This is like a beef burger, but way more special as it's made using pure beef and no binders. Use really good-quality mince but not too lean – you need some fat in there for juiciness and flavour. Jonti, my five-year-old son, just LOVES this and as it's full of protein it gives him loads of energy. This is a dinner straight out of my childhood; we used to eat it with a side of sautéed potatoes.

600 g minced beef
1 eschalot, finely chopped
2 tablespoons chopped chives, plus extra to serve
sea salt and freshly ground black pepper
2 tablespoons vegetable oil
40 g unsalted butter
4 eggs

1   Place the beef, eschalot and chives in a bowl, season to taste with salt and pepper and combine well. Divide the mixture into quarters and shape each quarter into a 10 cm round patty.

2   Heat the oil in a large heavy-based frying pan over high heat. Cook the patties for 3 minutes on each side or until golden and cooked to your liking. Remove from the pan and divide among serving plates.

3   Heat the butter in another large frying pan over medium heat. Carefully crack the eggs into the pan. Fry the eggs for 2 minutes, then reduce the heat to low, cover the pan and cook for another minute or until cooked to your liking. Place an egg on top of each beef patty, season to taste with salt and pepper, sprinkle with a little chopped chives and serve.

Serves 4 as a main

Hachis parmentier
FRENCH-STYLE COTTAGE PIE

You can start from scratch using raw minced beef here, but leftovers are really the way to go – so tasty (especially leftover Poached Beef in Broth on page 114 or Beef Cheek Bourguignon on page 102). This is quite a heavy dish and all it really needs as an accompaniment is a leafy green salad.

80 g unsalted butter, plus softened butter for greasing
1 onion, finely chopped
3 eschalots, finely chopped
2 cloves garlic, finely chopped
600 g minced beef or finely chopped leftover cooked beef, such
    as Poached Beef in Broth (see page 114) or Beef Cheek
    Bourguignon (see page 102)
1 large tomato, peeled (see page 209) and finely chopped
500 ml Brown Veal Stock (see page 47) or beef stock
1 kg brushed potatoes (such as sebago) or desiree potatoes
table salt
200 ml milk
2 eggs, 1 separated
sea salt and freshly ground black pepper
80 g breadcrumbs, made from day-old bread
1 tablespoon finely chopped thyme

1 Heat 20 g of the butter in a heavy-based saucepan over medium heat. When the butter starts to foam, add the onion, eschalot and garlic and stir for 4–5 minutes or until soft. Add the beef, tomato and stock. Bring to the boil, then reduce the heat to low and simmer for 20–25 minutes or until most of the liquid has evaporated. Remove from the heat and leave to stand until cool.

2 Meanwhile, peel the potatoes and cut them in half. Place in a saucepan of lightly salted water and bring to the boil over high heat, then reduce the heat to low and simmer for 20 minutes or until tender. Drain well, then return to the pan and shake over low heat to allow any excess moisture to evaporate. Push the potato through a fine-mesh sieve into a bowl, then add the milk, egg yolk and remaining butter and season to taste with salt and pepper.

3 Preheat the oven to 180°C and butter a 1.5 litre capacity shallow gratin dish well.

4 Season the meat mixture to taste with salt and pepper, then add 1 of the eggs and the egg white and combine well. Spoon the mixture into the prepared dish and smooth the top. Cover the meat with the mashed potato and sprinkle over the breadcrumbs mixed with the thyme.

5 Bake for 25 minutes or until the breadcrumbs are golden and crisp. Serve immediately.

Serves 6 as a main

Pot-au-feu
POACHED BEEF IN BROTH

Here's a perfect winter dish that uses all those lovely, inexpensive braising cuts of beef. Don't leave out the bone marrow; it gives a beautiful, lip-smacking flavour and it's so good for you! I adore *pot-au-feu* so much I'll often make double the recipe – that way there are leftovers to turn into a French-style cottage pie (see page 112). You can also blitz the leftover vegies and cooking liquid in the food processor to make a quick, tasty soup the next day.

1.5 kg mixed cuts of beef, including beef shank, oxtail and brisket
4 marrow bones
1 onion, halved
1 clove
1 clove garlic, bruised
1 bouquet garni (see page 208)
5 black peppercorns
1 teaspoon coarse sea salt
4 waxy potatoes, such as yukon gold or bintje (about 90 g each),
    halved lengthways
4 small carrots, halved lengthways and cut into 4 cm pieces
8 baby turnips, trimmed and halved lengthways
2 stalks celery, strings removed, halved lengthways and cut
    into 4 cm pieces
4 baby leeks, white part only, cut into 5 cm lengths
toasted sourdough, fleur de sel (see page 208), French wholegrain Dijon
    mustard (see page 208) and cornichons (see page 208), to serve

1   Place the meat and marrow bones in a large saucepan or stockpot and add enough cold water to cover well. Bring to a simmer over high heat and skim the impurities off the surface. As soon as the water starts to bubble (the water should never boil or the meat will toughen), reduce the heat to low. Add the onion, clove, garlic, bouquet garni and peppercorns. Simmer gently, skimming the surface regularly, for 1½ hours. Add the salt and cook for another 1½ hours or until the meat is very tender. You will need to check each type of meat for tenderness after 2 hours since they will take varying lengths of time to cook. (Oxtail will need up to 1 hour more than the other cuts to become tender.) Remove the meat from the pan and strain the broth through a fine-mesh sieve into a clean saucepan.

2   Bring the broth to the boil over medium heat. Add the potato and simmer gently for 5 minutes, then add the carrot and turnip and cook for 5 minutes. Add the leek and celery and cook for another 5 minutes or until all the vegetables are tender. (If you wish, you can divide the broth into thirds and cook the potatoes in one pan, the carrot and turnip in a second pan and the leek and celery in a third pan; the advantage of this is that you can better control the cooking of each vegetable.)

3   To serve, cut the meat into large pieces and remove the marrow from the bones. Spread the bone marrow over the toasted sourdough and serve the meat and some of the broth with fleur de sel, mustard and cornichons to the side.

Serves 4 as a main

Rôti de boeuf
ROAST BEEF

We French stole this from the English – and made it better! Some words of advice from Uncle Manu: don't season a big piece of meat like this with salt until after you've cooked it or the moisture will be drawn out. I also recommend that you don't cook your roast past medium–rare (use a meat thermometer if you're not sure – it should show 42°C) and let the roast rest for at least fifteen minutes before carving. That's how you cook perfect roast beef.

1 × 1 kg piece scotch fillet, beef rump or sirloin
4 cloves garlic, halved lengthways
60 ml vegetable oil
freshly ground black pepper
2 tablespoons chopped thyme
sea salt
125 ml red wine
250 ml Brown Chicken Stock (see page 46)
20 g cold unsalted butter, chopped

1   Remove the beef from the refrigerator 30 minutes before cooking.

2   Preheat the oven to 240°C.

3   Using a small sharp knife, make eight 2 cm deep incisions all over the beef. Push the garlic into the incisions. Rub the beef with a little of the oil, then season generously with pepper and sprinkle the thyme all over the top. Tie the beef into a compact shape with kitchen string at 5 cm intervals; this will assist it to roast more evenly.

4   Place the remaining oil in a heavy-based roasting pan over high heat. When the oil is very hot, cook the beef for 10–12 minutes or until golden all over; you want a deep golden colour. Transfer the pan to the oven and roast for 20 minutes for medium–rare, basting twice during cooking (or continue to roast until cooked to your liking).

5   Transfer the beef to a large shallow dish, season well with salt, cover loosely with foil and leave to rest in a warm place for 15 minutes.

6   Meanwhile, pour off the excess fat from the pan and place the pan over medium heat. Add the wine and use a wooden spoon to scrape any cooked-on bits from the base. Simmer the wine for 3–4 minutes or until it has reduced by half, then add the stock and combine well. Strain the sauce through a fine-mesh sieve into a small saucepan and simmer over low heat for 10 minutes or until reduced to a sauce consistency. Add any resting juices from the beef, then whisk in the butter, one piece at a time, and season to taste with salt and pepper.

7   To serve, cut the beef against the grain into 1 cm thick slices. Pour the sauce over the top and serve.

Serves 4 as a main

Tartare de boeuf
STEAK TARTARE

Steak tartare is a little like a Bloody Mary – you can adjust the spice and seasonings to your taste. Add more (or less), capers, Tabasco, Worcestershire sauce or whatever, as you like. And if you'd rather not use the raw egg yolk, you can 'cheat' by using homemade mayonnaise (see page 23) instead.

1 × 800 g piece beef fillet, eye fillet or rump steak
4 egg yolks
¼ cup finely chopped curly parsley
40 g cornichons (see page 208), finely chopped
30 g baby salted capers, rinsed very well and finely chopped
4 eschalots, finely chopped
Melba toasts, to serve

To your own taste:
tomato sauce
French Dijon mustard (see page 208)
Worcestershire sauce
Tabasco sauce
sea salt and freshly ground black pepper

1   Just before serving, use a large sharp knife to cut the beef into a very fine dice. (Don't be tempted to use a food processor as it will make a paste rather than dice. It is also ideal to chop the beef just before you intend to serve it to prevent it from oxidising.)

2   To serve, divide the meat into quarters, then shape each quarter into a neat mound on a serving plate. Make a shallow indent in the centre of each mound and carefully slide in an egg yolk, taking care not to break the yolk. Arrange the parsley, cornichons, capers and eschalot in separate piles around the plate and serve with tomato sauce, mustard, Worcestershire sauce, Tabasco and salt and pepper to the side. Your guests can season their steak to taste with their chosen condiments.

Serves 4

Côtes de veau aux morilles

VEAL CUTLETS WITH MOREL MUSHROOMS

Veal cutlets are much more expensive than escalopes, making this a rather refined sort of a meal – just make sure you source your veal from a really good butcher as there's a lot of dodgy veal out there that's tough and tasteless. I'd describe this as quite a restaurant-y dish with the cutlets and the morels – but even so, it's pretty easy to make. Cook it when you want to impress someone.

10 g dried morel mushrooms (see page 209)
100 ml warm water
4 veal cutlets (about 300 g each)
sea salt and freshly ground black pepper
1½ tablespoons vegetable oil
20 g unsalted butter
2 eschalots, finely chopped
60 ml dry white wine
150 ml Brown Chicken Stock (see page 46)
150 ml pouring cream
⅓ cup flat-leaf parsley, finely chopped

1   Soak the dried morels in the warm water for 15 minutes, then drain, reserving the water. Rinse the morels to remove any remaining grit, then thinly slice and set aside.

2   Season the veal on both sides with salt and pepper. Heat the oil and butter in a large heavy-based frying pan over medium heat. When the butter starts to foam, add the cutlets and cook for 2–3 minutes on each side or until golden, continuously spooning the fat over them. Holding the veal with tongs, cook the veal, fat-side down, for 5 minutes or until the fat is golden and melted. Place the veal on one side again and cook for another 1–2 minutes or until just cooked through. Transfer to a wire rack placed over a baking tray, cover loosely with foil and leave to rest in a warm place for 5 minutes.

3   Meanwhile, drain all but 1 tablespoon fat from the pan. Add the eschalot and cook over low heat for 3 minutes or until soft. Add the morels and cook for another 2 minutes, then add the wine and simmer until reduced by half. Add the stock, 60 ml of the strained reserved morel soaking water and the cream and simmer for 8–10 minutes or until reduced to the consistency of pouring cream. Season to taste with salt and pepper, then stir in the parsley and any juices from the resting veal and remove from the heat.

4   To serve, transfer the veal cutlets to plates and spoon the sauce over.

Serves 4 as a main

Blanquette de veau
CREAMY VEAL STEW

This reminds me of winter evenings at home in France. We'd smell Mum's veal simmering on the stove and know instantly that a delicious blanquette was on its way. I don't like flour-thickened sauces but this is one instance where flour works well. The best thing to serve this with is a rice pilaf (see page 144). The rice gets drenched in all that creamy, mushroomy goodness and it's just yum.

1.2 kg boned veal shoulder meat, trimmed
    and cut into 4–5 cm pieces
1 large carrot, quartered
1 large onion, quartered
1 leek, white part only, quartered
1 stalk celery, quartered
2 cloves garlic, bruised
1 sprig thyme
1 bay leaf
5 white peppercorns
1 clove
coarse sea salt
50 g unsalted butter
50 g plain flour

100 g creme fraiche
2 egg yolks
sea salt and freshly ground white pepper
pinch of freshly grated nutmeg
Rice Pilaf (see page 144), to serve

Garnish
300 g small pearl onions, trimmed
large pinch caster sugar
60 g unsalted butter, chopped
300 g button mushrooms, wiped clean and
    halved or quartered if large
sea salt and freshly ground black pepper

1 Place the veal in a large enamelled cast-iron casserole and add enough water to cover well. Bring to the boil over high heat and skim the impurities from the surface. Reduce the heat to as low as possible (use a simmer mat if necessary) and add the carrot, onion, leek, celery, garlic, thyme, bay leaf, peppercorns, clove and a pinch of coarse sea salt. Cover with a tight-fitting lid and simmer, skimming regularly, for 1½ hours or until the meat is very tender.

2 Meanwhile, to prepare the garnish, place the onions, sugar, 30 g of the butter and a pinch of salt and pepper in a small saucepan. Pour in enough water to come halfway up the sides of the onions. Bring to the boil over medium heat, then cover and cook for 10 minutes. Remove the lid and cook for another 5 minutes or until all the water has evaporated and the onions are tender, lightly coloured and glazed. Remove from the heat and set aside. Heat the remaining butter in a large frying pan over medium heat. When the butter starts to foam, add the mushrooms and cook for 5–6 minutes or until golden and tender. Remove from the heat and season to taste with salt and pepper.

3 Drain the veal in a colander placed over a large saucepan. Discard the cooking vegetables, herbs and spices, then cover the meat loosely with foil and set aside. Simmer the cooking liquid over medium heat for 20 minutes or until reduced to 1 litre. Melt the butter in a saucepan over low heat. When the butter starts to foam, add the flour and stir for 2 minutes or until the mixture becomes 'sandy'. Gradually add the hot reduced cooking liquid to the pan, whisking continuously until smooth and well combined. Simmer for 10 minutes, then remove from the heat. Combine the creme fraiche and egg yolks in a small bowl, then whisk into the hot sauce until well combined. Season to taste with salt, pepper and nutmeg.

4 Transfer the veal, mushrooms and glazed onions to the sauce and stir gently to combine and warm through. Serve immediately with rice pilaf.

Serves 4 as a main

Escalope de veau Viennoise
VEAL ESCALOPES VIENNA

Buy good-quality veal escalopes from a reputable butcher to make this simple dish shine. The best crumbs to use are the ones you make yourself, although the Japanese variety panko, that are now readily available in larger supermarkets, will do in a pinch. The combo of crunchy crumbs, tender veal and that salty hit of anchovy and capers plus tart lemon to cut through the oil is just brilliant.

4 veal escalopes (about 200 g each)
sea salt and freshly ground black pepper
plain flour, seasoned with salt and pepper, for dusting
2 eggs, lightly beaten
150 g fine breadcrumbs, made from day-old bread
50 ml vegetable oil
20 g unsalted butter
½ lemon
lemon slices, anchovy fillets (see page 208) and black olives
    (optional), to serve

Egg and caper sauce
2 eggs
30 g salted capers, rinsed well and chopped
½ cup flat-leaf parsley, finely chopped
4 anchovy fillets (see page 208), finely chopped
extra virgin olive oil

1   To make the egg and caper sauce, place the eggs in a small saucepan, cover with cold water and bring to the boil over medium heat. Cook for 8 minutes for hard-boiled, then drain and refresh in cold water. Shell the eggs, then separate the whites and yolks and finely chop. Set the yolk and white aside in separate bowls.

2   Lightly beat the veal escalopes with the flat side of a meat mallet or a rolling pin until they are of an even thickness. Season the veal with salt and pepper on both sides. Place the flour, beaten eggs and breadcrumbs in separate shallow bowls. Dust the veal in flour, shaking off the excess. Dip in the beaten egg, then coat in the breadcrumbs.

3   Heat the oil and butter in a large heavy-based frying pan over medium–high heat. When the butter starts to foam, add the crumbed veal and cook for 2 minutes on each side or until golden and cooked through. Squeeze the lemon juice into the oil and butter mixture and spoon over the veal. Remove the veal from the pan and drain on paper towel.

4   Combine the egg yolk, egg white, capers, parsley, and anchovy in a small bowl, then drizzle in enough olive oil to moisten.

5   To serve, divide the veal among serving plates, then spoon over a little of the egg and caper sauce. Top with a slice of lemon and an olive wrapped in an anchovy fillet, if desired.

Serves 4 as a main

Jarret de veau braisé au vin rouge
BRAISED VEAL SHANKS WITH RED WINE

I came across a similar recipe in a book once and loved it – I've just tweaked it a little to reflect me. The shanks and sauce cook until the meat is almost falling off the bone and the sauce is reduced until it is sticky and sweet; I adore this kind of food. The juniper and cinnamon aren't very French, although they do use those spices a bit down in the south of the country. The balsamic vinegar definitely isn't French, but who cares, it makes the sauce taste fantastic!

2 tablespoons olive oil
60 g cold unsalted butter, chopped
4 veal shanks (about 500 g each), French-trimmed (see page 209)
1 onion, cut into 2 cm pieces
1 carrot, cut into 2 cm pieces
1 leek, white part only, cut into 2 cm pieces
2 cloves garlic, bruised
375 ml red wine
1 litre Brown Chicken Stock (see page 46)
3 sprigs thyme
2 sprigs rosemary
1 cinnamon stick
10 juniper berries
125 ml balsamic vinegar
steamed double-peeled broad beans (optional), to serve

1   Preheat the oven to 180°C.

2   Heat the olive oil and 20 g of the butter in a large enamelled cast-iron casserole over medium heat. When the butter starts to foam, add the shanks and cook for 5 minutes or until browned all over. Remove the veal from the pan, then add the onion, carrot, leek and garlic and stir for 6–8 minutes or until golden.

3   Return the shanks to the pan, then add the wine and bring to the boil. Add the stock, thyme, rosemary, cinnamon, juniper berries and balsamic vinegar. Bring to the boil again, cover with a piece of baking paper (cartouche, see page 208), then seal with a lid and bake, turning the shanks once, for 2 hours or until the meat almost falls of the bone.

4   Remove the shanks from the sauce, then strain the sauce through a fine-mesh sieve into a clean pan, pressing down on the solids with the back of a ladle to extract as much flavour as possible. Simmer the sauce for 20 minutes or until it has reduced by half, then whisk in the remaining 40 g butter, one piece at a time.

5   To serve, check the seasoning of the sauce, then pour it over the shanks and scatter with broad beans, if desired.

Serves 4 as a main

Escalope de veau à la Normande

VEAL ESCALOPES WITH MUSHROOMS AND CREAM

Normandy, in the very north of France, is famous for producing apples and apple products, hence the apple brandy, Calvados, in this recipe. This is another childhood favourite of mine and I've found it's a good dish to make when you want to introduce kids to mushrooms. When I was growing up, Mum would serve it with a side of tagliatelle, and that's still how I prefer to eat it.

50 g unsalted butter, chopped
200 g button mushrooms, wiped clean and quartered
sea salt and freshly ground black pepper
4 veal escalopes (about 180 g each)
1 tablespoon vegetable oil
50 ml Calvados
150 ml Brown Chicken Stock (see page 46)
150 ml pouring cream

1   Melt 20 g of the butter in a large heavy-based frying pan over high heat. When the butter starts to foam, add the mushrooms and cook for 3 minutes or until just soft and golden. Season the mushrooms to taste with salt and pepper, then remove from the pan and set aside.

2   Season the veal with salt and pepper on both sides. Heat the oil and remaining 30 g butter in the frying pan over high heat. When the butter starts to foam, add the veal and cook for 2 minutes on each side. Transfer the veal to a plate and cover loosely with foil, then leave to rest in a warm place.

3   Meanwhile, pour off the excess fat from the pan and return the pan to medium heat. Add the Calvados and stock and bring to the boil, then add the cream. Reduce the heat to low and simmer for 8–10 minutes or until the sauce has reached the consistency of pouring cream. Add the mushrooms and simmer for another 3 minutes, then season to taste with salt and pepper and remove from the heat.

4   To serve, transfer the veal escalopes to plates and spoon the sauce over.

Serves 4 as a main

Côtes de porc charcutière
PORK CUTLETS WITH MUSTARD AND CORNICHONS

The mustard flavour here is mellow because it's Dijon. Make sure you use French mustard here (and in all the recipes in the book that call for it), never English, American or, that stuff called 'French-style'. They're not the same and some commercial mustards are just plain bad. Serve the cutlets with a good, lighter style red wine (Beaujolais or pinot noir) and a side of mash.

4 pork cutlets (about 250 g each), French-trimmed (see page 209)
sea salt and freshly ground black pepper
2 tablespoons vegetable oil
40 g unsalted butter, chopped
3 eschalots, finely chopped
1 tablespoon French Dijon mustard (see page 208)
100 ml dry white wine
150 ml Brown Chicken Stock (see page 46)
1 tablespoon tomato paste
5 large cornichons (see page 208), cut into julienne (see page 209)
¼ cup finely chopped curly parsley

1   Season the pork to taste on both sides with salt and pepper. Heat the oil and butter in a large heavy-based frying pan over medium heat. When the butter starts to foam, add the pork and cook for 2–3 minutes on each side or until golden. Reduce the heat to low and cook for another 3–4 minutes on each side or until just cooked through. (The cooking time will vary depending on the thickness of your cutlets.) Put the pork onto a wire rack placed over a baking tray near the stove. Set aside to rest.

2   Return the pan to low heat and add the eschalot, then stir for 2–3 minutes or until soft. Add the mustard and stir for 2 minutes. Increase the heat to medium, then add the wine and scrape the base of the pan with a wooden spoon to remove any cooked-on bits. Simmer for 3–4 minutes or until reduced by half, then add the stock and tomato paste and continue to simmer until reduced by half again. Stir in the cornichons, parsley and any resting juices from the pork and season to taste with salt and pepper.

3   To serve, transfer the pork cutlets to plates, then spoon the sauce over.

Serves 4 as a main

Rôti de porc aux pruneaux 'façon mère Badet'

POT-ROASTED PORK WITH PRUNES 'MOTHER BADET'S WAY'

One day I was talking to my chef Alban about roast pork. Like me, he's from Brittany, and he said, 'Oh my mum's roast pork with prunes is to die for!' I asked him to cook it for me and he did. I just loved it and asked him to let me use the recipe in my book. He said *mais oui*, so here it is.

1 × 1 kg pork belly, boned and skin removed, then
    rolled and tied at 2 cm intervals
sea salt and freshly ground black pepper
1½ tablespoons olive oil
30 g unsalted butter
1 onion, finely chopped
2 cloves garlic, finely chopped
150 ml dry white wine
150 ml Brown Chicken Stock (see page 46)
200 g prunes, pitted
1 sprig thyme
1 bay leaf
Green Beans with Morel Mushroom Butter (optional,
    see page 144), to serve

1   Preheat the oven to 190°C.

2   Season the pork all over with salt and pepper. Heat the olive oil in an enamelled cast-iron casserole just large enough to fit the pork. Cook the pork over high heat, turning for 10 minutes or until browned all over; it's important to get a good colour on the pork to seal in the moisture. Remove the pork from the pan, then discard the fat and wipe the pan clean.

3   Return the pan to low heat and add the butter. When the butter starts to foam, add the onion and garlic and cook for 7–8 minutes or until golden. Add the wine and stock and bring to the boil. Return the pork to the pan, then add the prunes, thyme and bay leaf (I tie these together with kitchen string) and cover with a tight-fitting lid. Roast the pork for 1 hour or until it is cooked through and tender – try not to open the lid during cooking!

4   Remove the pork from the pan and transfer to a large plate, then leave to rest in a warm place for 15 minutes. Remove the thyme and bay leaf from the pan, then adjust the seasoning with salt and pepper. Bring the pan juices to a simmer just before serving.

5   To serve, slice the pork, divide among plates and spoon the prunes and sauce over. Serve with green beans with morel mushroom butter, if desired.

Serves 4 as a main

Tomates farcies
STUFFED TOMATOES

At home, growing up, Mum would serve this in the winter using big, fat, juicy tomatoes from the south of France. It's quite a filling dish really, especially if you serve it with plenty of bread to dunk in the pan juices. While I use minced pork, you could use a combination of pork and beef mince or just all beef, if you prefer.

8 vine-ripened tomatoes
1 tablespoon sea salt
1 tablespoon olive oil, plus extra for drizzling
½ onion, finely chopped
1 clove garlic, finely chopped
250 g minced pork
1 egg
½ cup flat-leaf parsley leaves, finely chopped
50 g dried breadcrumbs
freshly ground black pepper
pinch of freshly grated nutmeg

1   Trim the bases of the tomatoes so they stand upright; take care not to make any holes in the bases or the juices will leak out during cooking. Cut the tops off to make lids. Using a teaspoon, scoop out the seeds from the bases and tops, discarding the seeds. Sprinkle the bases and tops with salt and stand, cut-side down, on a tea towel for 15 minutes to draw out any excess liquid.

2   Meanwhile, heat the olive oil in a heavy-based saucepan over low heat. Add the onion and garlic and cook, stirring occasionally, for 5 minutes or until soft but not coloured. Remove from the heat and leave to cool.

3   Preheat the oven to 180°C.

4   Place the minced pork, egg, parsley, breadcrumbs and cooled onion mixture in a large bowl. Season to taste with salt, pepper and nutmeg, then use clean hands to combine very well.

5   Turn the tomatoes upright and place in a roasting pan. Divide the stuffing among the tomatoes, then top with the tomato lids. Drizzle with a little olive oil and roast for 30 minutes or until golden and tender.

6   Serve warm.

Serves 4 as a main

Côtes de porc Dijonnaise

PORK CUTLETS WITH CREAMY MUSTARD SAUCE

The flavours in this are zingy and summery – all those cornichons and mustard really wake up your taste buds. The meat is definitely a feature here so use great-quality pork from a reputable butcher if you can and, as the dish is on the rich side, just serve this with a crisp green salad.

4 pork cutlets (about 250 g each), French-trimmed (see page 209)
sea salt and freshly ground black pepper
1½ tablespoons vegetable oil
30 g unsalted butter
2 cloves garlic, finely chopped
2 eschalots, finely chopped
150 ml dry white wine
150 ml Brown Chicken Stock (see page 46)
150 ml pouring cream
50 g French Dijon mustard (see page 208)
30 g wholegrain Dijon mustard (see page 208)
1 sprig thyme, leaves picked, plus thyme sprigs (optional), to serve

1   Season the pork cutlets on both sides with salt and pepper. Heat the oil and butter in a large heavy-based frying pan over medium heat. When the butter starts to foam, add the pork and cook, continuously spooning the fat over the top, for 4–5 minutes on each side or until golden. Holding the pork with tongs, cook the pork fat-side down for 5 minutes or until the fat is melted and golden. Continue to turn the pork on each side and cook for another 1–2 minutes or until just cooked through. Put the pork onto a wire rack placed over a baking tray, cover loosely with foil and rest in a warm place.

2   Meanwhile, drain all but 1 tablespoon of the fat from the pan and place the pan over low heat. Add the garlic and eschalot and cook for 2–3 minutes or until just soft. Add the wine, then increase the heat to medium–high and simmer for 3–4 minutes or until reduced by half. Add the stock and cream and simmer for 8 minutes or until reduced by half again. Whisk in the mustards and any juices from the resting pork and add the thyme. Season the pork to taste with salt and pepper and remove the pan from the heat.

3   To serve, transfer the pork cutlets to plates, then spoon the sauce over. Scatter with extra thyme sprigs, if desired.

Serves 4 as a main

Gratin d'endives au jambon
BAKED WITLOF AND HAM GRATIN

Out of all my mum's recipes, this one is at the top of my list of favourites. It might sound strange to braise witlof because in Australia it is mostly used as a salad green – but trust me, this is unbelievably good. Its creamy, ham-infused sauce and crusty cheesy top make it irresistible. Make sure the witlof is well cooked; there should be no resistance when you cut it.

6 witlof
75 g soft unsalted butter
large pinch of caster sugar
sea salt and freshly ground white pepper
1 onion, finely chopped
2 cloves garlic, finely chopped
300 ml White Chicken Stock (see page 46)
150 ml pouring cream
15 g plain flour
3 thin slices leg ham, cut in half
50 g gruyerè, grated

1   Remove and reserve the outer leaves from the witlof. Trim the bases, taking care not to remove too much or the witlof will fall apart during cooking. Finely chop the outer leaves. Set aside.

2   Heat 60 g of the butter over medium heat in an enamelled cast-iron casserole just large enough to fit the witlof in a single layer. When the butter starts to foam, add the whole witlof, then sprinkle with the sugar and season to taste with salt and pepper. Turn for 3–4 minutes or until light golden on all sides, then add the onion, garlic, stock and chopped witlof. Reduce the heat to low, then cover and cook the witlof for 25–30 minutes or until tender.

3   Meanwhile, preheat the oven to 180°C.

4   Carefully remove the witlof from the pan, allowing as much cooking liquid as possible to drain off them. Drain well on paper towel to remove as much moisture as possible.

5   Strain the cooking liquid through a fine-mesh sieve into a small saucepan. Add the cream and simmer over low heat for 8–10 minutes or until it is reduced by half. Combine the flour and remaining 15 g butter in a small bowl. Whisking continuously, add the flour and butter mixture to the reduced cooking liquid and simmer for 5 minutes or until the sauce is thickened and smooth. Remove the pan from the heat and season the sauce to taste with salt and pepper.

6   Wrap each witlof in half a slice of ham and place in a shallow baking dish just large enough to hold them, close together, in a single layer. Pour over the sauce and sprinkle with the grated cheese. Bake the gratin for 20 minutes or until it is golden and bubbling. Serve.

Serves 6 as a light meal

Petit salé aux lentilles
SMOKED PORK HOCK WITH GREEN LENTILS

Here's a real winter dish that's excellent reheated the next day when all the flavours have had time to mingle and infuse. Leftovers can be turned into soup with the addition of some stock – just take the ham off the bone (it should be falling off anyway) and chop up the speck and big pieces of veg before you reheat it all. Or puree it in the style of the lentil and speck soup on page 60.

1 onion, halved
2 cloves
2 large smoked pork hocks
3 carrots, 2 halved lengthways, 1 finely chopped
2 sprigs thyme
2 bay leaves
5 black peppercorns
150 g green Puy-style lentils
1.25 litres water
3 cloves garlic, bruised
coarse sea salt and freshly ground black pepper
1 × 100 g piece speck (see page 209), cut into
    3 cm × 1 cm strips (lardons, see page 209)
8 spring onions, trimmed and cut into 3 cm lengths
½ cup flat-leaf parsley, chopped
extra virgin olive oil, for drizzling

1   Stud each onion half with a clove. Place the pork hocks in a large saucepan and cover well with cold water. Bring to the boil over high heat. Reduce the heat to low, then add a studded onion half, one of the halved carrots, 1 thyme sprig, 1 bay leaf and the peppercorns. Simmer gently for 2 hours.

2   Meanwhile, 1 hour before the hocks are ready, place the lentils in a saucepan with the water and bring to the boil over medium–high heat. Add the remaining studded onion half, the remaining halved carrot, garlic, thyme sprig and bay leaf. Reduce the heat to low and simmer for 25 minutes. Season the lentils to taste with coarse sea salt and cook for another 15 minutes or until tender. Drain the lentils well, then remove and discard the onion, carrot, garlic and herbs and return the lentils to the pan.

3   Heat a large frying pan over high heat and cook the speck for 4–5 minutes or until golden. Reduce the heat to low, then add the spring onion and stir for another 5 minutes. Add the chopped carrot to the pan and cook for 4–5 minutes or until tender, then remove from the heat. Transfer the speck mixture and parsley to the lentils, then season to taste with salt and pepper.

4   Drain the pork hocks and, when cool enough to handle, remove and discard the skin and bones, if desired.

5   To serve, divide the lentils among bowls or serving plates, then top with pieces of pork hock and a good drizzle of extra virgin olive oil.

Serves 4 as a main

Carré d'agneau persillé
HERB-CRUSTED RACK OF LAMB

Aussie lamb is beautiful and, if you can get saltbush lamb, so much the better! We have the same thing back home in France, where it's called *pre-salé* lamb, and the one from Brittany is quite famous. Cook your lamb until it is medium–rare and let it rest for fifteen minutes so it stays juicy and pink inside.

80 g fine breadcrumbs, made from day-old bread
2 small cloves garlic, finely chopped
1 cup curly parsley, finely chopped
1 teaspoon chopped thyme
sea salt and freshly ground black pepper
15 g unsalted butter, melted
1 × 8-cutlet rack of lamb (approximately 500 g),
    French-trimmed (see page 209)
1 tablespoon olive oil
10 eschalots, peeled
2 tablespoons French Dijon mustard (see page 208)
Braised Peas with Lettuce and Speck (optional, see page 146), to serve

1   Preheat the oven to 180°C.

2   Place the breadcrumbs, garlic, parsley and thyme in a bowl, then season to taste with salt and pepper and combine well. Stir in the melted butter until the mixture starts to come together to form a paste.

3   Using a sharp knife, score the fat of the lamb rack on the diagonal at 2 cm intervals. Wrap the ends of the bones with foil to prevent them burning. Season the meat all over with salt and pepper.

4   Heat the olive oil in a flameproof roasting pan over medium heat and pan-fry the lamb and eschalots for 6–8 minutes or until golden brown. Transfer the pan to the oven and roast the lamb, fat-side up, for 7 minutes, then remove from the oven.

5   Working quickly, spread the mustard over the scored fat-side of the lamb, then press the breadcrumb mixture over the top in an even layer. Return to the oven and roast the lamb for another 5 minutes or until the crust is golden and crisp; the meat will still be pink inside. Remove the lamb from the oven and rest in a warm place for 15 minutes before carving.

6   To serve, remove the foil, then carve the lamb rack into portions and divide among plates. Serve with braised peas with lettuce and speck, if desired.

Serves 4 as a main

Navarin d'agneau
LAMB NAVARIN

Traditionally this was served in spring as a transitional dish between winter and summer. Even though it's a braise, it's quite light, with all those lovely sweet, baby spring vegies in it. Not to mention the lamb shoulder – lamb in spring tastes just brilliant and this is a great way to make the most of it.

50 ml olive oil
1 kg boneless lamb shoulder, cut into
    4–5 cm pieces
sea salt and freshly ground black pepper
1 onion, cut into 1 cm pieces
1 carrot, cut into 1 cm pieces
30 g plain flour
2 cloves garlic, bruised
4 tomatoes, cut into 8 wedges each
3 sprigs thyme
1 bay leaf
100 ml dry white wine
1 litre White Chicken Stock (see page 46)
finely chopped curly parsley (optional), to serve

Garnish
12 salad onions, green parts trimmed
    and bases left whole with the root
    ends intact
45 g unsalted butter
pinch caster sugar
250 ml White Chicken Stock (see page 46),
    approximately
12 baby carrots, peeled and trimmed
12 baby turnips, peeled and trimmed

1   Heat the olive oil in a large enamelled cast-iron casserole over high heat. Working in batches, cook the lamb for 5 minutes or until golden all over, then season to taste with salt and pepper. Remove the lamb from the pan and set aside. Add the onion and carrot to the pan and stir for 2 minutes or until lightly coloured. Return the lamb to the pan, sprinkle over the flour and stir for 2 minutes.

2   Add the garlic, tomato, thyme, bay leaf, wine and stock to the pan. Bring to the boil, then reduce the heat to low, partially cover with a lid to allow steam to escape and simmer for 50 minutes.

3   Meanwhile, to make the garnish, place the onions, 15 g of the butter and a pinch each of sugar, salt and pepper in a small saucepan and pour in enough stock to come halfway up the side of the onions, then cover and cook over medium heat for 10 minutes. Remove the lid and cook for another 5 minutes or until all the liquid has evaporated and the onions are lightly coloured and tender when pierced with a small sharp knife. Remove from the heat and set aside. Repeat in separate pans with the remaining butter, carrots, turnips and stock. The carrots will take about 8 minutes and the turnips will take about 12 minutes to cook, so check and remove them from the heat as soon as they are tender.

4   Drain the lamb in a colander sitting over a large bowl and reserve the broth. Wash and dry the casserole and return the lamb to it. Using a ladle, remove the fat from the top of the broth, then pour the broth through a fine-mesh sieve back over the lamb. Simmer the lamb over low heat for another 20–25 minutes or until tender. Check the seasoning, then add the glazed onions, carrots and turnips and simmer for another 2 minutes.

5   To serve, scatter the lamb navarin with parsley, if desired, and divide among shallow bowls or plates.

Serves 4 as a main

Gigot d'agneau braisé
BRAISED LAMB SHOULDER

This makes a perfect Sunday lunch – if you can wake up early enough in the morning to get it cooking. You can use either leg or shoulder, it doesn't really matter. This dish goes perfectly with Roasted Tomatoes with Thyme (see page 144) and a simple green salad served as accompaniments.

1 × 1.5 kg shoulder of lamb
sea salt and freshly ground black pepper
50 ml vegetable oil
1 carrot, cut into 1 cm pieces
1 onion, cut into 1 cm pieces
3 teaspoons tomato paste
4 cloves garlic, peeled
1 bay leaf
2 sprigs thyme
50 ml dry white wine
200 ml Brown Veal Stock (see page 47) or beef stock
Roasted Tomatoes with Thyme (optional, see page 144), to serve

1 Preheat the oven to 130°C.

2 Season the lamb generously with salt and pepper. Heat the oil in a flameproof roasting pan or large enamelled cast-iron casserole over medium–high heat. Cook the lamb for 8–10 minutes or until browned all over, then remove from the pan. Add the carrot and onion and cook for 6–7 minutes or until golden. Add the tomato paste, garlic, bay leaf and thyme and stir to combine well. Return the lamb to the pan, then add the wine and stock and bring to the boil.

3 Cover the pan with foil or a tight-fitting lid and roast the lamb for 3 hours or until it is very tender and nearly falling off the bone. Remove the lamb from the pan and season the sauce with salt and pepper to taste.

4 To serve, carve the lamb and divide among plates, then spoon the sauce over. Serve with roasted tomatoes, if desired.

Serves 4–6 as a main

Haricots verts aux beurre de morilles
GREEN BEANS WITH MOREL MUSHROOM BUTTER

This is a really good way to dress up plain green beans. Keep the butter in the freezer, so that you always have some on hand, then cut off pieces with a heated knife when you wish to use it.

10 g dried morel mushrooms (see page 209)
100 ml hot water
1½ tablespoons olive oil
2 eschalots, finely chopped
1 clove garlic, finely chopped
80 g unsalted butter, chopped, at room temperature
sea salt and freshly ground black pepper
600 g green beans, trimmed
1 tablespoon finely chopped chives

Place the morels and hot water in a small bowl and leave to stand for 15 minutes. Drain the morels and rinse well to remove any excess grit from the mushrooms. Coarsely chop and set aside.

Heat the olive oil in a large frying pan over medium heat. Cook the eschalot for 2 minutes or until soft but not coloured. Add the garlic and cook for another minute, then stir in the morels. Remove from the heat and set aside to cool.

Combine the cooled morel mixture and butter in a bowl and season to taste with salt and pepper. Spread the mixture on a piece of plastic film. Roll up the log, twist the ends to seal, then roll the log back and forth on the bench-top to make it firm. Refrigerate until needed or freeze for up to 1 month.

Cook the beans in a pan of lightly salted boiling water for 3 minutes or until tender but still firm to the bite. Drain well.

Heat the morel butter in a large frying pan over medium heat. When the butter starts to foam, add the hot beans and chives and toss to coat well. Season to taste with salt and pepper and serve immediately.

Serves 4

Tomates à la Provençale
ROASTED TOMATOES WITH THYME

4 large ripe tomatoes, halved widthways
80 ml olive oil
sea salt and freshly ground black pepper
50 g coarse breadcrumbs, made from day-old bread
¼ cup chopped curly parsley
1 tablespoon thyme, chopped
2 cloves garlic, finely chopped

Preheat the oven to 170°C. If necessary, cut a little off the base of the tomatoes so they stand upright. (Be careful not to cut through the flesh or the juices will escape.) Place the tomatoes, cut-side up, in a shallow baking dish. Drizzle with the olive oil and season with salt and pepper. Process the breadcrumbs, parsley, thyme and garlic in a small food processor until well combined. Divide the breadcrumb mixture evenly among the tomatoes and bake for 30 minutes or until the tops are golden. Serve.

Serves 4

Riz pilaf
RICE PILAF

500 ml White Chicken Stock (see page 46)
1½ tablespoons vegetable oil
1 small onion, finely chopped
300 g long-grain rice
sea salt and freshly ground black pepper
1 bay leaf

Preheat the oven to 180°C. Bring the chicken stock to the boil in a saucepan; keep warm. Heat the oil in a deep ovenproof saucepan over low–medium heat, then cook the onion, stirring frequently, for 10 minutes or until just golden brown. Add the rice to the pan and season to taste with salt and pepper, then stir to coat with the onion mixture. Pour the hot stock over the rice, add the bay leaf then cover. Cook in the oven for 20 minutes. Remove the pan from the oven, then leave to rest for at least 10 minutes (or up to 1 hour). Fluff the rice with a fork, then serve.

Serves 4

Flan de courgettes
ZUCCHINI FLANS

Kids love this way with zucchini and it's very easy to whip up. It is a really versatile side dish that goes especially well with fish.

4 green zucchini (about 150 g each)
50 ml olive oil, plus extra for greasing
3 eschalots, finely chopped
2 eggs
100 ml pouring cream
freshly grated nutmeg
sea salt and freshly ground black pepper

Preheat the oven to 180°C.

Wash and coarsely grate the zucchini and gently squeeze between your hands to remove any excess liquid.

Heat the olive oil in a heavy-based frying pan over medium heat. Add the eschalot and stir for 1–2 minutes or until soft. Add the zucchini and stir for 4–5 minutes or until it is just cooked and all the liquid has evaporated. Transfer to a blender and process until smooth. Leave in the blender for 5 minutes or until slightly cooled. Add the eggs and cream, season to taste with nutmeg, salt and pepper and process until well combined.

Pour the mixture into four lightly greased 250 ml capacity ramekins and place in a deep roasting pan. Pour in enough hot water to come two-thirds of the way up the sides of the ramekins, then bake for 30 minutes or until the zucchini mixture is just set.

Carefully remove the roasting pan from the oven, then run a small knife around the inside of the ramekins to loosen the flans. Invert onto plates and serve.

Serves 4

Pommes dauphines
POTATO CROQUETTES

Not the quickest of things to make but they are just so delicious that I can never stop eating them! Use an ice-cream scoop to make them into perfect rounds, then drop directly into a pan of hot oil and voila!

500 g brushed potatoes such as sebago, halved or
    quartered if large
table salt
1 egg
2 egg yolks
freshly grated nutmeg
sea salt and freshly ground white pepper
vegetable oil, for deep-frying

Choux pastry
60 ml water
60 ml milk
50 g unsalted butter, chopped
75 g plain flour
2 eggs

To make the choux pastry, place the water, milk and butter in a saucepan over high heat. As soon as the mixture comes to just below the boil, remove from the heat and stir in the flour all in one go. Beat with a wooden spoon for 1 minute or until the mixture comes together. Place the hot choux mixture in the bowl of an electric mixer and beat with the paddle attachment for 1–2 minutes to allow some of the heat to escape. With the motor running, add the eggs, one at a time; allow each one to be fully incorporated before adding the next. (The mixture should be glossy and smooth.) Transfer to a bowl, cover closely with plastic film and leave until cooled to room temperature.

Meanwhile, place the potato in a large saucepan of lightly salted water and bring to the boil. Reduce the heat to medium and simmer for 15 minutes or until tender. Drain well, then, using the back of a large metal spoon or a pastry scraper, push the hot potato through a fine-mesh sieve into a large bowl. Add the egg and egg yolks, season to taste with nutmeg, salt and pepper and combine well. Stir in the choux pastry until well combined, then season again if necessary.

Heat the oil in a large heavy-based saucepan or domestic deep-fryer to 160°C. Using two dessertspoons or a small ice-cream scoop, shape the dough into small balls and cook, in batches, turning for 5–6 minutes or until golden and puffed. Drain on paper towel and serve hot.

Serves 6

Petits pois à la Française

BRAISED PEAS WITH LETTUCE AND SPECK

It might sound strange to braise lettuce but trust me, when slow-cooked with salty bacon and sweet peas, it tastes amazing. Peas are often treated so plainly and when you cook them this way you'll see them in a whole new light. Here they are like little explosions of sweetness.

1 × 250 g piece speck (see page 209), cut into
    3 cm × 1 cm strips (lardons, see page 209)
½ bunch small spring onions, trimmed and halved
50 g unsalted butter, chopped
½ iceberg lettuce, outer leaves removed and discarded,
    cored and finely shredded
500 g frozen peas
60 ml White Chicken Stock (see page 46)
sea salt and freshly ground black pepper

Heat a large deep frying pan over medium heat. Add the speck and cook, stirring regularly, for 4–5 minutes or until golden. Add the spring onions and butter and stir for another 3–4 minutes or until the onions are tender.

Add the lettuce to the pan and stir until wilted, then add the peas and stock and season to taste with salt and pepper. Increase the heat to medium–high and simmer rapidly for 10 minutes or until the vegetables are tender, the liquid has reduced and its flavour has become more concentrated. Check the seasoning and serve.

Serves 6

Gratin de chou-fleur

CAULIFLOWER GRATIN

This is the ultimate vegie dish to go with a roast, whether it is beef, lamb or chicken. I would never dish up a pile of plain old boiled cauliflower – how horrible! In France we make a feature of vegetables, turning them into a proper finished dish because we believe that everything we make should be cooked with care and love.

1 small head cauliflower (about 1 kg), core removed,
    broken into florets
table salt
1 quantity hot Bechamel Sauce (see page 98)
250 g gruyère cheese, grated
4 egg yolks
sea salt and freshly ground white pepper
soft unsalted butter, for greasing

Preheat the oven to 200°C.

Drop the cauliflower into a saucepan of lightly salted boiling water and simmer for 8–10 minutes or until just tender. Drain and set aside.

Meanwhile, while the bechamel is still hot, stir in 100 g of the grated cheese and the egg yolks and season to taste with salt and pepper if necessary.

Grease a shallow 1 litre capacity baking dish with butter, then spread the cauliflower over the base. Pour over the bechamel, then sprinkle with the remaining cheese. Place on a baking tray and bake for 15–20 minutes or until golden brown. Serve.

Serves 6

Pommes de terre salardaise
CRISPY DUCK-FAT FRIED POTATOES

This originates from the South-West of France, where they make a lot of confit, so there's always plenty of duck fat on hand. Duck fat is easy to buy now in tins from specialty food stores.

550 g small desiree potatoes, cut into 5 mm thick slices
table salt
100 g duck fat
2 eschalots, thinly sliced
2 cloves garlic, finely chopped
¼ cup finely chopped curly parsley
sea salt and freshly ground black pepper

Place the potato in a saucepan of lightly salted water. Bring to the boil over medium heat, then remove from the heat and leave the potato to stand in the water for 15 minutes. The potato should be half-cooked. Drain the potato in a colander, then spread on a clean tea towel in a single layer and pat dry.

Heat the duck fat in a large heavy-based frying pan over medium heat. Add half of the potato slices and cook for 3–4 minutes on each side or until golden. Remove with tongs and repeat with the remaining potato. Return all the potato to the pan, then add the eschalot and turn for 2 minutes or until it is just soft. Add the garlic, parsley and salt and pepper to taste, then toss for 1 minute or until the garlic is just fragrant. Serve immediately.

Serves 4

Gratin dauphinois
POTATO GRATIN

This is a beautiful potato cake, it's just so creamy. You can really expand on this by adding different herbs, maybe a little bacon or, if you can get them, truffles. Another option is to replace half of the potatoes with another root vegetable such as parsnip or sweet potato. For best results I recommend using a mandoline to thinly slice the potatoes.

500 ml pouring cream
1 clove garlic, finely chopped
1 tablespoon chopped thyme
1 kg brushed potatoes (such as sebago) or desiree potatoes, peeled and cut into 3 mm thick rounds
sea salt and freshly ground black pepper
20 g unsalted butter

Combine the cream, garlic, thyme and potato in a large heavy-based saucepan, then season to taste with salt and pepper. Bring to the boil, then reduce the heat to low and simmer for 10 minutes, stirring gently to prevent the potato from sticking to the base of the pan.

Meanwhile, preheat the oven to 180°C. Grease a 1.5 litre capacity baking dish with the butter.

Transfer the potato and cream mixture to the baking dish, spreading it into an even layer. Cover with foil, then bake for 1½ hours or until the potato is tender. Remove the foil and bake for another 10 minutes or until the top of the potato is golden brown and all the cream is absorbed.

Serve immediately.

Serves 4

Poulet rôti à l'estragon de Maman
MUM'S ROAST CHICKEN WITH TARRAGON

Sometimes a dried herb is better than a fresh one; the long cooking here will simply kill the flavour of fresh tarragon. As a general rule, fresh herbs are best when they are added to a dish right at the very end of cooking so their flavours and colour remain bright. Serve this with cauliflower gratin (see page 146) for the ultimate (that is, my mum's) roast chook.

125 g soft unsalted butter
1 tablespoon dried tarragon
1 × 1.8 kg chicken
sea salt and freshly ground black pepper
2 onions, cut into wedges
6 cloves garlic
Cauliflower Gratin (optional, see page 146), to serve

1   Preheat the oven to 190°C.

2   Place the butter and tarragon in a small bowl and combine well. Using your fingers and starting at the neck end of the chicken, gently ease the skin away from the breast, taking care not to pierce the skin. Evenly spread one-third of the tarragon butter between the flesh and skin of each side of the breast; take care not to tear the skin. Spread the remaining tarragon butter over the top of the chicken and season inside and out with salt and pepper. Truss the chicken with kitchen twine and place on its side in a roasting pan.

3   Roast the chicken for 15 minutes, then turn onto the other side. Roast for another 15 minutes, then turn the chicken, breast-side up. Add the onion and garlic to the pan and cook for another 20–30 minutes or until the chicken is cooked through, basting frequently – the chicken is ready when the juices from the thigh joint run clear when pierced with a skewer.

4   Remove the chicken from the oven and place, breast-side down, in a warm bowl. Cover loosely with foil and leave to rest for 10 minutes before carving.

5   To serve, carve the chicken and divide among plates. Serve with cauliflower gratin, if desired.

Serves 4 as a main

Poulet Basquaise
BASQUE-STYLE CHICKEN STEW

This summery dish features the flavours of the Basque region – capsicum and a type of chilli called espelette. In this part of France you can see houses covered with these chillies drying in the sun. This recipe is inspired by my great friend and fellow chef Jean Francois. He is from the Basque country and owns the charming restaurant Le Pelican in Surry Hills, Sydney.

100 ml olive oil
2 onions, halved lengthways and thinly sliced
4 cloves garlic, crushed
100 g prosciutto, cut into 4 cm long × 3 mm thick
    strips (batons, see page 208)
1 each red, yellow and green capsicum (pepper), trimmed,
    seeded and cut into 4 cm long × 3 mm thick strips
    (batons, see page 208)
2 fresh long green chillies, halved, seeded and cut into
    4 cm long × 3 mm thick strips (batons, see page 208)
cayenne or Espelette chilli pepper (see page 208), to taste
1 sprig thyme
1 bay leaf
3 large tomatoes, peeled (see page 209), seeded and
    finely chopped
200 ml dry white wine
50 ml red-wine vinegar
sea salt and freshly ground black pepper
4 chicken marylands (leg and thigh joints)
Rice Pilaf (optional, see page 144), to serve

1   Heat 50 ml of the olive oil in a large saucepan over medium heat. Add the onion and stir for
    3–4 minutes or until soft but not coloured. Add the garlic and prosciutto and cook, stirring regularly
    for 10 minutes. Add the capsicum, chilli and cayenne pepper and cook for another 5 minutes or until
    the capsicum is just soft. Add the thyme, bay leaf, tomato and wine, then simmer for 6–8 minutes or
    until reduced by two-thirds. Pour in the vinegar and continue to simmer for 5 minutes or until nearly all
    the wine and vinegar have evaporated. Season to taste with salt and pepper and set aside.

2   Meanwhile, season the chicken all over with salt and pepper. Heat the remaining 50 ml olive oil in a large
    enamelled cast-iron casserole over medium–high heat. Cook the chicken, turning for 5–6 minutes or until
    browned all over, then cover the pan, reduce the heat to low and cook for 20 minutes.

3   Spread the vegetable mixture over the chicken. Cover and cook over low heat for another 50–60 minutes
    or until the chicken is very tender and nearly falling off the bone. Check the seasoning and serve with
    rice pilaf, if desired.

Serves 4 as a main

Poule au pot
POACHED CHICKEN IN BROTH

If you are feeling rich you can slide sliced truffles under the skin of the chicken (the ones from Western Australia are really good!). If you have any leftovers, I suggest pureeing the vegetables in the stock for a quick soup and chopping up the leftover cold meat to use in the juiciest chicken mayo sandwiches.

1 × 2 kg free-range chicken
large pinch coarse sea salt
1 onion, cut into wedges
2 sprigs thyme
1 bay leaf
5 black peppercorns
1 clove
3 cloves garlic
olive oil, for brushing

Garnish
14 baby carrots, peeled and trimmed
8 baby turnips, peeled and trimmed
8 baby leeks, trimmed, washed well and cut
       into 10 cm lengths
4 Brussels sprouts, halved

1   Place the chicken in a large saucepan. Add the salt and enough cold water to cover well. Bring to the boil over high heat, then add the onion, thyme, bay leaf, peppercorns, clove and garlic. Reduce the heat to low and simmer for 1 hour or until the chicken is just cooked.

2   After 45 minutes, remove 750 ml of the stock from the pan and place in a saucepan. Bring to the boil and, working in batches, separately cook the carrots and turnips for 10 minutes, and leeks and Brussels sprouts for 5 minutes until just tender. (They will all take differing amounts of time to cook.) As they are cooked, place on a warm shallow dish and cover with foil.

3   To serve, remove the chicken from the broth and place on a large serving platter. Remove the skin and brush the flesh with a little olive oil, then cut the chicken into pieces. Serve the hot poached vegetables around the side of the chicken, with the broth served separately.

Serves 4 as a main

Magret de canard au poivre vert

PAN-ROASTED DUCK BREASTS WITH GREEN PEPPERCORN SAUCE

This is a beautiful classic French recipe, great for impressing family and friends (and making you look like a real chef). The sauce has a little bit of a kick to it, but is so delicious that I always want more. The trick with duck is to cook it so that the fat renders well as this makes the skin nice and crisp – take care not to overcook it as the meat will dry out. It should be nicely pink and juicy in the centre.

4 duck breast fillets (about 180 g each), skin on
sea salt and freshly ground black pepper
50 g unsalted butter
4 eschalots, finely chopped
2 tablespoons drained green peppercorns in brine
2 tablespoons Madeira
1½ tablespoons French Dijon mustard (see page 208)
300 ml Brown Chicken Stock (see page 46)
200 ml pouring cream
Potato Gratin (optional, see page 147), to serve

1   Season the skin of each duck breast generously with salt and pepper, rubbing it in well; this helps to release the fat and make the skin crisp. Season the flesh side.

2   Heat a large heavy-based frying pan over medium heat – it is not necessary to add oil as the duck skin will release sufficient fat. Cook the duck breasts, skin-side down, for 6–8 minutes or until the skin is very crisp and golden and most of the fat has rendered. Turn the breasts and cook for another 5 minutes; the breasts should still be pink in the middle; the cooking time will vary depending on the thickness of the duck breasts. Transfer the duck to a plate, skin-side up. Cover loosely with foil and stand in a warm place while you make the sauce.

3   Drain the fat from the pan, then add the butter, eschalot and peppercorns and cook over low heat for 3–4 minutes or until soft. Increase the heat to medium–high and add the Madeira. Use a wooden spoon to scrape the bottom of the pan to remove any cooked-on pieces. Whisk in the mustard, then add the stock and bring to the boil. Add the cream and bring to the boil again. Reduce the heat to low and simmer for 6–8 minutes or until reduced to a sauce consistency. Check the seasoning.

4   To serve, slice the duck breasts and divide among plates, then spoon the green peppercorn sauce over the top. Serve with potato gratin, if desired.

Serves 4 as a main

Confit de canard
DUCK CONFIT

Confit is easy to make but the salting of the duck is really important so don't skip this step. This curing process draws out moisture and flavours the meat – you can't season it afterwards. When you want to serve the confit, just remove the duck from the fat, then place it under the griller to crisp the skin. Good confit should be crunchy on the outside and moist on the inside. Duck fat is readily available from specialty food stores.

200 g coarse sea salt
1 clove garlic
2 cloves
5 black peppercorns
1 star anise
finely grated zest of 1 orange

1 sprig thyme
1 bay leaf
4 duck marylands (leg and thigh joints)
1 kg duck fat
chopped thyme and Crispy Duck-fat Fried Potatoes
    (optional, see page 147), to serve

1   Place the salt, garlic, cloves, peppercorns, star anise, orange zest, thyme and bay leaf in food processor and pulse briefly until well combined.

2   Place the duck marylands in a deep ceramic baking dish large enough to hold them snugly in one layer, then add the salt mixture and toss to coat well. Cover with plastic film and refrigerate for 3 hours.

3   Remove the duck from the salt mixture, wiping away the excess with paper towel. Rinse well under cold water, then pat dry on a clean tea towel.

4   Place the duck fat in a large enamelled cast-iron casserole and heat over very low heat until melted. Add the duck legs and cook for 2 hours or until the meat is very tender and starting to come away from the bone. It is important to cook the duck as slowly as possible – the temperature of the fat should not exceed 80°C on a candy/deep-fry thermometer (see page 208).

5   Preheat the oven to 200°C. Remove the duck from the fat and put, skin-side up, onto a wire rack placed over a baking tray. Roast the duck for 5–10 minutes or until the skin is golden and crisp, then serve, scattered with thyme (if using), with fried potatoes alongside, if desired.

Serves 4 as a main

TIPS AND TRICKS

*   If you want to make the confit in advance and store it in fat, in order to have sufficient fat to cover the duck you will need to use additional fresh duck fat to the fat that the duck was cooked in. Melt another 1 kg duck fat and pour a 2 cm layer into a sterilised container. Once the fat has cooled and set, add the cooked duck legs, cover with the remaining fat, making sure all the duck is covered, then leave to cool completely. Seal tightly and refrigerate for up to 2 months. To serve, carefully remove the duck from the fat, wipe off the excess fat, then heat in a 200°C oven for 5–10 minutes.
*   You can store the duck fat you cooked the duck in in the refrigerator for up to 3 months and use it for roasting or sautéing potatoes (see Crispy Duck-fat Fried Potatoes, page 147).

Cailles aux raisins
QUAIL WITH RAISINS

The quail is a small bird with lots to say – especially after it has been drinking brandy! The marriage between sweet raisins and pink gamey meat is seriously good, especially when you cook it so the skin turns golden and caramelised. Don't bother with cutlery when serving this dish; it tastes best when you dig in and use your fingers.

150 g raisins
200 ml hot water
6 quail (about 190 g each)
sea salt and freshly ground black pepper
1 tablespoon vegetable oil
70 g cold unsalted butter, chopped
2 sprigs thyme
60 ml brandy
500 ml Brown Chicken Stock (see page 46)
2 teaspoons sherry vinegar (see page 209)
finely chopped chives (optional), to serve

1   Preheat the oven to 180°C.

2   Place the raisins and hot water in a bowl and leave to stand for at least 15 minutes to plump. Drain and set aside.

3   Meanwhile, pat the quail dry with paper towel, then season inside and out with salt and pepper. Heat the oil, 30 g of the butter and the thyme in a saute pan or enamelled cast-iron casserole over high heat. When the butter starts to foam, cook the quail, turning for 4–5 minutes or until browned all over.

4   Cover the pan with a lid, then transfer to the oven and roast for 10 minutes or until just cooked through. Remove the quail from the pan and place in a wide serving dish.

5   Add the raisins to the pan and stir over medium heat for 5 minutes. Add the brandy and simmer until reduced by half. Increase the heat to high, then add the stock and simmer for a few minutes or until reduced by half. Reduce the heat to low and whisk in the remaining 40 g butter until the sauce is glossy and slightly thickened; do not boil. Whisk in the vinegar and check the seasoning. Return the quail to the pan and baste them in the sauce, then scatter with chives, if desired.

6   To serve, divide the quail among serving plates, then spoon the sauce over.

Serves 6

Lapin chasseur
BRAISED RABBIT WITH SPECK AND MUSHROOMS

Rabbit has very lean meat and, even though this is a braised dish, you need to be careful not to overcook it or the rabbit will dry out. You could also make this exact same dish using chicken. Either way, the best thing to serve it with is a rich mash or creamy polenta.

1 × 1.6 kg rabbit
sea salt and freshly ground black pepper
50 ml vegetable oil
40 g unsalted butter, chopped
200 g speck (see page 209), diced
250 g button mushrooms, wiped clean and
    halved or quartered if large
2 eschalots, thinly sliced
4 cloves garlic, finely chopped
2 sprigs thyme
1 bay leaf
50 ml brandy
50 ml dry white wine
700 ml Brown Chicken Stock (see page 46)
¼ cup coarsely chopped french tarragon
    (optional), to serve

1   Using a sharp knife, cut the front and back legs from the rabbit. Remove the sinew from the saddle meat and cut the saddle into 4 pieces, leaving the meat on the bone (or ask your butcher to do this). Season the rabbit pieces with salt and pepper.

2   Heat the oil and 20 g of the butter in a large enamelled cast-iron casserole over medium heat. When the butter starts to foam, add the rabbit pieces and cook for 3 minutes on each side or until golden. Remove the rabbit from the pan and set aside. Add the remaining butter and the speck and mushrooms to the pan and stir for 4–5 minutes or until golden, then remove from the pan. Add the eschalot, garlic, thyme and bay leaf and stir for 1–2 minutes or until fragrant.

3   Return the rabbit forelegs and hind legs to the pan, then add the brandy and carefully tilt the pan towards the flame to ignite the alcohol (or use a lighter if necessary). When the flames have subsided, add the wine and simmer until reduced by half. Add the stock and bring to the boil, then reduce the heat to low, cover closely with a piece of baking paper (cartouche, see page 208), then a lid and simmer over very low heat (use a simmer mat if necessary) for 45 minutes. Add the saddle pieces and simmer for another 10 minutes or until just cooked through. Remove the rabbit pieces from the pan and set aside.

4   Strain the cooking liquid through a fine-mesh sieve into a large saucepan and simmer over medium heat for 10 minutes or until reduced by half. Season to taste, then add the mushrooms and rabbit. Simmer the rabbit for 1–2 minutes or until just warmed through.

5   To serve, scatter the rabbit with tarragon, if desired, and divide among plates.

Serves 4 as a main

Lapin à la moutarde
BRAISED RABBIT WITH MUSTARD SAUCE

This is Mum's classic way with rabbit. My auntie's mum and dad farmed rabbits and when we wanted one for the table they'd simply go and grab one from the hutch and kill it on the spot right in front of us – it was the freshest rabbit ever. This is a robust dish that is best served in winter.

50 ml vegetable oil
20 g unsalted butter
4 rabbit hind-legs (order in advance from your butcher)
sea salt and freshly ground black pepper
120 g French Dijon mustard (see page 208)
3 teaspoons thyme leaves
2 eschalots, thinly sliced
150 ml dry white wine
250 ml pouring cream
chopped thyme and fresh fettucine or tagliatelle, to serve

1   Preheat the oven to 160°C.

2   Heat the oil and butter in an enamelled cast-iron casserole over medium heat. When the butter starts to foam, add the rabbit legs, season to taste with salt and pepper and cook for 6 minutes or until golden on both sides. Remove the pan from the heat, then remove the legs from the pan and spread with a little of the mustard, sprinkle with thyme leaves and set aside.

3   Return the pan to the heat. Add the eschalot and stir over low heat for 3 minutes or until soft. Add the wine and bring to the boil. Return the rabbit to the pan and cover with a tight-fitting lid.

4   Transfer the rabbit to the oven and bake, rotating the legs twice during cooking, for 45 minutes or until tender.

5   Remove the rabbit from the pan and place on a large serving plate. Return the pan to the heat, then add the cream and the remaining mustard and stir well to remove any cooked pieces on the bottom of the pan. Simmer the mixture over low heat for 5–6 minutes or until it is reduced by one-third. Check the seasoning and adjust with more salt and pepper if desired.

6   To serve, pour the mustard sauce over the rabbit, scatter with thyme and serve with fettucine or tagliatelle.

Serves 4 as a main

DESSERTS

Tarte tatin de Maman

MUM'S UPSIDE-DOWN CARAMELISED APPLE TART

This is the only one of Mum's recipes I can never replicate exactly. Her tarte tatin is the best on the planet – she's made it so many times. At the restaurant we serve this with creme fraiche as the tart is so sweet and the tanginess of the creme fraiche cuts through the sweetness a little. I say 'no' when people ask to have it with ice cream!

100 g caster sugar
1 vanilla pod, seeds scraped
60 g unsalted butter, chopped
4–5 Fuji apples
1 quantity Shortcrust Pastry (see page 206)
plain flour, for dusting
creme fraiche or sour cream, to serve

1   Preheat the oven to 190°C.

2   Peel, quarter and core the apples. Place a 25 cm heavy-based ovenproof frying pan (a cast-iron pan is ideal) over medium heat. Add the sugar and cook over low heat, tilting the pan occasionally until a golden caramel forms; do not stir. Sprinkle over the vanilla seeds and 20 g of the butter and allow to bubble up, then swirl the pan several times to combine well. Remove from the heat.

3   Place the apples in the pan, rounded-side down and tightly packed, starting from the outside and working your way into the centre. Dot with the remaining butter, then return to the heat and simmer, gently shaking the pan occasionally to prevent any burnt spots, for 5–6 minutes or until a dark rich caramel forms and bubbles up around the apples. Remove from the heat.

4   Roll out the pastry on a lightly floured surface into a round just a little larger than the frying pan. Place the pastry on top of the apple and tuck the pastry down around the apple against the edge of the pan – as if you're tucking a blanket in around the apples. Bake the tart for 30 minutes or until the pastry is golden and cooked and you can see caramel bubbling around the sides.

5   Remove the pan from the oven and leave the tart to stand in the pan to cool for 1 hour. (If you don't allow the tart to cool down before you turn it out, the apple can stick to the base, so be patient!)

6   Just before serving, place a large plate over the top of the pan and invert the pan in one smooth movement so the pan is now on top. Lift off the pan to reveal the tart, then slice the tart and serve with big dollops of creme fraiche or sour cream.

Serves 8

Pain perdu
FRENCH TOAST

I do love the non-French version of this for breakfast with bacon and maple syrup. In France *pain perdu* was originally served as a dessert made from leftover bread that people didn't want to waste. Now we just make it because it is delicious. Only use a proper, buttery brioche from a good baker. For a breakfast version of French toast, you could use sourdough bread instead of brioche.

500 ml milk
pinch ground cinnamon
60 g caster sugar
2 eggs
4 thick slices stale brioche (the brioche needs
    to be a couple of days old)
60 ml clarified butter (see page 208)
jam or vanilla bean ice cream, to serve

1 Place the milk, cinnamon and 30 g of the sugar in a wide flat dish and whisk until well combined. Soak the brioche in the milk mixture for 2–3 minutes. Meanwhile, place the eggs in a wide shallow bowl and whisk until lightly beaten.

2 Heat a large non-stick frying pan over medium heat. Add half of the clarified butter and the remaining 30 g sugar and cook until melted and well combined. Dip 2 slices of the soaked brioche into the beaten egg to coat well, then fry in the butter and sugar mixture for 2–3 minutes on each side or until golden. Wipe the pan clean, then repeat with the remaining butter, brioche and egg and serve hot with jam or vanilla bean ice cream.

Serves 4

Crème brûlée
VANILLA BEAN CREME BRULEE

It doesn't matter what else is on the dessert menu at the restaurant, if there is creme brulee it just walks out the door. It's hard to beat – with its lovely rich custard and crunchy caramel topping, the combination of textures is truly spectacular. It's actually a very simple recipe but probably one of the hardest to get right. To caramelise the sugar properly you need to use either a domestic blowtorch (see page 208) or a brulee iron. Don't try to use the oven griller, it won't work.

500 ml pouring cream
1 vanilla pod, seeds scraped
5 egg yolks
90 g caster sugar

1 Place the cream, vanilla seeds and the pod in a saucepan and simmer over low heat for 10 minutes. Remove from the heat and leave to stand for 1 hour to infuse. Strain the cream through a fine-mesh sieve into a jug and discard the vanilla pod.

2 Place the egg yolks and 50 g of the sugar in a large bowl and whisk until just well combined. Slowly stir in the warm cream until just combined; do not stir too vigorously as you do not want to create bubbles in the custard. (At this stage, you can cover the custard closely with plastic film and refrigerate overnight to enhance the flavour and then remove any bubbles which may have formed on the surface of the custard before cooking.)

3 Preheat the oven to 120°C.

4 Place four 150 ml capacity brulee dishes or ramekins in a deep roasting pan. Carefully divide the custard among the dishes, then place the pan in the oven. Pour enough boiling water into the pan to come halfway up the side of the dishes. Bake the custards for 30–40 minutes or until just set. The cooking time will depend on the depth of the dishes – the custards should still be a little wobbly in the centre.

5 Carefully remove the roasting pan from the oven, then remove the dishes from the water bath and set aside to cool. Cover the brulees with plastic film, then refrigerate for at least 6 hours or overnight.

6 Just before serving, sprinkle the surface of each brulee with 2 teaspoons of the remaining sugar, using the back of a teaspoon to spread it evenly. Using a kitchen blowtorch (see page 208), melt and caramelise the sugar. The sugar should be dark golden but not burnt. Serve immediately.

Serves 4

Tarte au citron meringuée
LEMON MERINGUE TART

My grandfather was a pastry chef and, when I was a child, everything he made looked so enticing that it seemed as though even his shop window was edible! I recommend making your own pastry – you will really taste the difference. This is my mum's favourite dessert (even though she prefers it without the meringue). You can flavour the curd with orange for a change but you'll need to keep some of the lemon juice in there or the curd won't have that nice zing.

⅔ quantity Sweet Shortcrust Pastry
   (see page 206)
plain flour, for dusting
4 egg whites
220 g caster sugar

Lemon curd filling
150 g unsalted butter, chopped
6 eggs
180 g icing sugar, sifted
300 ml freshly squeezed lemon juice, strained

1   Roll out the pastry on a lightly floured surface to 4 mm thick, then use to line a 25 cm tart tin with a removable base. Use a small sharp knife to trim off the excess pastry. Prick the pastry base all over with a fork, then refrigerate for 1 hour.

2   Preheat the oven to 190°C.

3   Place a piece of baking paper over the pastry, then fill with pastry weights, dried beans or rice, place the tart tin on a baking tray and bake for 10–15 minutes or until the pastry is light golden.

4   Remove the weights or beans and the paper, then reduce the temperature to 180°C and bake the pastry for another 10 minutes or until the base is dry. Remove from the oven and set aside to cool.

5   Reduce the oven temperature to 130°C.

6   To make the lemon curd filling, melt the butter in a small saucepan over low heat. Place the eggs and icing sugar in a large heatproof bowl and whisk until well combined. Add the lemon juice, then slowly whisk in the melted butter. Place the bowl over a saucepan of just simmering water, making sure the bottom of the bowl does not touch the water, and whisk for 10 minutes or until the curd has the consistency of thick cream.

7   Pour the lemon filling into the cooled tart shell and bake for 15 minutes or until the filling is just set. Remove the tart from the oven.

8   Increase the oven temperature to 220°C.

9   Using an electric mixer, whisk the egg whites until soft peaks form. Gradually add the sugar and whisk until thick and glossy. Spoon the mixture into a piping bag fitted with a large plain nozzle and pipe over the top of the tart. (Alternatively, spoon the mixture on top of the tart and spread with a spatula to make irregular peaks.) Bake the tart for 3–4 minutes or until the meringue is just golden. Remove from the oven and leave to stand until just cool, then serve.

Serves 8

Pêche Melba
PEACH MELBA

This dessert was created by the famous French chef Escoffier in 1893 for Dame Nellie Melba, the renowned Australian opera singer. Originally it was considered a fancy restaurant dessert but now it's widely made at home as well as it's so easy. All the elements are simple but they need to be fresh – no tinned peaches, please!

150 g caster sugar
500 ml water
½ vanilla pod, seeds scraped
2 ripe yellow slipstone peaches
125 g raspberries, plus extra to serve
300 g vanilla bean ice cream
1 quantity Chantilly Cream (see page 207)
50 g flaked almonds, toasted (see page 209)
mint sprigs, to serve

1 Place the sugar, water, vanilla seeds and the pod in a heavy-based saucepan and stir over low heat until the sugar dissolves. Increase the heat to medium and bring to the boil.

2 Meanwhile, cut the peaches in half and remove the stones. Add the peach halves to the syrup, then cover with a piece of baking paper (cartouche, see page 208). Reduce the heat to low and poach gently for 20 minutes. Remove the pan from the heat and leave the peaches to cool in the syrup, then refrigerate until cold. Drain the peaches, reserve the liquid and remove the skins.

3 Place the raspberries and 30 ml of the cooled syrup in a blender and process until smooth. Strain through a fine-mesh sieve sitting over a bowl and refrigerate until needed.

4 Several hours before serving, place 4 serving glasses in the freezer to chill.

5 To serve, place a scoop of ice cream in each serving glass, then top with a peach half, cut side-down. Coat the peaches with the raspberry sauce (coulis), top with a little Chantilly cream, some flaked almonds, extra raspberries and a mint sprig and serve immediately.

Serves 4

Mousse au chocolat noir
DARK CHOCOLATE MOUSSE

This recipe comes from my days as an apprentice chef and I have made it so many times it is completely ingrained in my memory. I can whip it up with my eyes shut. I like to serve it with palmiers as their crispness is the perfect counterpoint to the silkiness of the mousse. It's hard to go wrong when making this, although you do need to use a decent quality chocolate. You can splash a little Cointreau into the mix for an orange edge if you like.

250 g dark couverture chocolate (66% cocoa solids, see page 208), chopped
50 g unsalted butter, chopped
1 egg yolk
7 egg whites
50 g caster sugar
100 g dark couverture chocolate, for grating

Palmiers
1 egg yolk
1 tablespoon water
1 sheet butter puff pastry, thawed
plain flour, for dusting
90 g icing sugar, plus extra for dusting

1   Place the chocolate and butter in a heatproof bowl over a saucepan of just simmering water, then stir frequently until melted and smooth. Remove the bowl from the heat, then add the egg yolk and stir until smooth.

2   Using an electric mixer, whisk the egg whites until just foamy. Gradually add the sugar, then continue to beat until soft peaks form; do not overbeat the egg whites or the mousse will be grainy. Gently fold one-third of the egg whites into the chocolate mixture to loosen, then fold in the remaining egg whites until well combined. Spoon the mixture into a 1.25 litre capacity serving bowl or six 200 ml capacity glasses, cover with plastic film and refrigerate overnight.

3   Meanwhile, for the palmiers, preheat the oven to 180°C.

4   Place the egg and water in a bowl and stir to combine. Place a pastry sheet on a lightly floured chopping board. Brush the pastry with the egg mixture, then sift over 2 tablespoons of the icing sugar. Starting from one side, roll up the pastry to form a long cigar-shape. Repeat with the remaining pastry and another 2 tablespoons of the sugar.

5   Cut the pastry 'cigars' into 1 cm thick rounds. Dust a work surface with icing sugar, then top with a pastry round. Dust the top of the pastry round with more icing sugar, then use a rolling pin to roll into a long thin oval (about 8–10 cm long). Transfer to a baking tray lined with baking paper. Repeat with the remaining pastry rounds and icing sugar. Bake for 12–15 minutes or until golden. Transfer to a wire rack to cool. (Makes about 18 palmiers. Leftovers can be stored in an airtight container for up to 7 days.)

6   To serve, hold the extra chocolate in your hand to gently warm, then grate the chocolate over the top of the mousse. Serve with palmiers to the side.

Serves 6

Tartelettes aux framboises
RASPBERRY TARTLETS

Mmmm, these and a glass of champagne – perfection! Fruit tarts are another French classic that never need to be played around with or 'improved'. How can you make the combination of homemade sweet pastry, gorgeous creme patissiere and fresh berries any better? Well, okay, you could glaze the tops – melt some berry jam and sieve it, then brush it while still warm over the berries to make them gleam (see opposite).

1 quantity Sweet Shortcrust Pastry (see page 206)
plain flour, for dusting
375 g raspberries
icing sugar (optional), for dusting

Creme patissiere
500 ml milk
1 vanilla pod, seeds scraped
6 egg yolks
100 g caster sugar
45 g plain flour

1   To make the creme patissiere, place the milk and vanilla seeds and the pod in a heavy-based saucepan over medium heat. Bring to just below the boil, then remove from the heat. Strain the milk through a fine-mesh sieve into a jug and set aside to cool until just warm.

2   Place the egg yolks and sugar in a large bowl and whisk until thick and pale. Add the flour and combine well. Whisk in half of the warm milk until well combined, then whisk in the remaining milk. Transfer the mixture to a non-stick saucepan and stir over low–medium heat for 2–3 minutes until the mixture comes to the boil, then whisk for another 2–3 minutes or until thick and smooth. Transfer the creme patissiere to a cold bowl, then place a piece of plastic film directly on top so that it is touching it – this prevents a skin forming. Leave the creme patissiere to cool to room temperature, then refrigerate until cold.

3   Meanwhile, roll out the pastry on a lightly floured surface until 4 mm thick and use to line six 12 cm tart tins with removable bases. Use a small sharp knife to trim off the excess. Prick the pastry bases with a fork. Refrigerate for 1 hour.

4   Preheat the oven to 180°C.

5   Line the base and side of each pastry shell with a piece of baking paper, then fill with pastry weights, dried beans or rice. Place the tart tins on a baking tray and bake for 15 minutes or until the pastry is light golden. Remove the baking tray from the oven, remove the weights and paper and return the pastry shells to the oven to bake for another 5 minutes or until the pastry is golden and dry. Remove the pastry shells from the oven and place on a wire rack to cool completely.

6   Spoon the creme patissiere into a piping bag fitted with a 1.5 cm wide nozzle, then pipe it evenly into the cooled tart shells. Place the raspberries on top and dust with icing sugar, if desired. Serve.

Serves 6

Poires Belle Hélène
POACHED PEARS WITH CHOCOLATE SAUCE

Pears and chocolate are a classic marriage and this is another dessert, invented in 1870, by the renowned French chef Escoffier. It was named after an Offenbach operetta called *La Belle Hélène*. This is just the quickest dessert on earth to pull together. You can poach the pears up to two days in advance and make the sauce at the last minute. Too easy.

½ vanilla pod, seeds scraped
1 litre water
200 g caster sugar
4 williams pears
½ lemon
150 g dark couverture chocolate (66% cocoa solids,
    see page 208), chopped
300 g vanilla bean ice cream
1 quantity Chantilly Cream (see page 207)
20 g flaked almonds, toasted (see page 209)

1   Place the vanilla seeds and pod, water and sugar in a saucepan just large enough to hold the pears and stir over low heat until the sugar dissolves. Bring to the boil, then remove the pan from the heat.

2   Peel the pears, rubbing the peeled surface with the cut lemon as you go to prevent them from browning. Add the pears to the sugar syrup, cover with a piece of baking paper (cartouche, see page 208) and simmer over low heat for 20 minutes or until a skewer inserted into a pear withdraws easily. Remove the pan from the heat and leave the pears to cool in the syrup.

3   Drain the pears and reserve the syrup. Using a teaspoon and working from the base of each pear, scoop out the core and seeds and discard.

4   To make the chocolate sauce, place 150 ml of the reserved syrup in a small saucepan over low heat and bring to just below a simmer. Place the chocolate in a heatproof bowl, pour over the hot syrup and stir until the chocolate is melted and smooth.

5   To serve, divide the pears among 4 serving glasses and pour over the chocolate sauce. Place a small scoop of ice cream to the side of the pears, then pipe a little Chantilly cream into the glasses. Sprinkle the cream with flaked almonds, then serve immediately.

Serves 4

Tarte soufflée au chocolat
CHOCOLATE TART SOUFFLE

This recipe was given to me by my friend and former collegue Jeremie Mantelin, who is a brilliant pastry chef. This is the easiest tart. All you do is make the pastry, melt the chocolate, whip up the sabayon, knock it together, stick it in the oven and that's it! The filling puffs up then sinks when it cools and the middle is nice and gooey.

1 quantity Chocolate Shortcrust Pastry (see page 207)
plain flour, for dusting
450 g dark couverture chocolate (66 % cocoa solids,
     see page 208), chopped
225 g unsalted butter, chopped
3 eggs
6 egg yolks
150 g caster sugar
creme fraiche, to serve

1   Roll out the pastry on a lightly floured benchtop, lifting, turning and dusting the bench as you go, until the pastry is 4 mm thick and large enough to line the base and sides of a 25 cm tart tin with a removable base. Use a small sharp knife to trim off any excess pastry. Prick the pastry base all over with a fork, then refrigerate for 30 minutes.

2   Preheat the oven to 190°C.

3   Line the pastry shell with baking paper, then fill with pastry weights, dried beans or rice and bake for 15 minutes. Reduce the oven temperature to 180°C, then remove the weights and paper and cook the tart shell for another 5 minutes or until it is dry.

4   Meanwhile, heat the chocolate and butter in a heatproof bowl over a saucepan of just simmering water, stirring occasionally, until the chocolate and butter are melted and smooth; take care that the bottom of the bowl does not touch the water. Remove from the heat, reserve the pan of simmering water and leave the chocolate mixture to stand until cooled to room temperature.

5   Place the eggs, yolks and sugar in another large heatproof bowl and place over the saucepan of just simmering water. Using a whisk (a balloon whisk is ideal), whisk until the mixture holds a trail. Remove the pan from the heat, then gradually whisk the cooled chocolate mixture into the egg mixture and combine well.

6   Pour the chocolate mixture into the tart shell and bake for 18–20 minutes or until just set; the tart should be nice and gooey. Leave the tart to cool to room temperature, then serve with spoonfuls of creme fraiche.

Serves 8

Îles flottantes
FLOATING ISLANDS

These meringues should be like little clouds that just melt in your mouth; this is one of the first desserts that I ever made as an apprentice chef and it's still one of my all-time favourites. I promise you, once you make your own, proper egg custard (*crème anglaise*, see page 207) you'll never look at that bought stuff in tetra packs again.

vegetable oil, for brushing
200 ml egg whites (approximately 6 egg whites
    from 59 g eggs)
180 g caster sugar
50 ml water
300 ml Custard Cream (see page 207)
50 g flaked almonds, toasted (see page 209)
icing sugar, for dusting

1 Preheat the oven to 120°C.

2 Lightly grease six 200 ml capacity ramekins with oil and set aside.

3 Using an electric mixer, whisk the egg whites until soft peaks form, then gradually add 80 g of the sugar and whisk until stiff peaks form. Spoon the meringue into a piping bag fitted with a wide nozzle and pipe into the ramekins. Place the filled ramekins in a deep roasting pan and fill with enough boiling water to come halfway up the sides of the ramekins. Bake the meringues for 15–20 minutes or until lightly browned. Carefully remove the roasting pan from the oven and leave the ramekins to stand in the water bath until cool.

4 Meanwhile, place the water and remaining 100 g sugar in a small heavy-based saucepan and stir over low heat until the sugar dissolves. Bring to the boil and simmer, tilting the pan occasionally and brushing the inside of the pan frequently with a pastry brush dipped in cold water to dissolve any crystals, for 8–10 minutes or until a golden caramel forms. Do not stir. Remove from the heat and carefully add 2 tablespoons cold water – take care as the mixture will spit. Swirl to combine, then set aside to cool.

5 To serve, pour a little of the caramel sauce into the base of 6 serving glasses or dishes, then divide the custard cream among them and place a floating island on top. Drizzle with more of the caramel sauce and scatter with the almonds, then dust with icing sugar and serve immediately, with extra caramel sauce in a jug and extra toasted almonds to the side.

Serves 6

Riz au lait
CREAMY RICE PUDDING

Forget all you know about rice pudding. The French version, which includes whipped cream and *crème anglaise* (see page 207), is elegant and light. It should be served ever-so-slightly chilled. I think that if rice pudding is warm when you have it, it's like eating porridge. If you like, you could also make a light caramel to pour over the base of the ramekins before spooning in the rice pudding (similar to lining a mould for creme caramel). You could also stir a small handful of raisins into the rice after it has cooked, before placing it in the ramekins to chill.

125 g arborio rice
table salt
400 ml milk
75 g caster sugar
50 ml pouring cream
150 ml Custard Cream (see page 207)

1   Preheat the oven to 160°C.

2   Place the rice in a sieve and rinse under cold running water. Bring a saucepan of lightly salted water to the boil, then add the rice and simmer for 5 minutes. Drain the rice and refresh under cold water to stop it from cooking further.

3   Place the milk, sugar and a pinch of salt in an ovenproof saucepan and stir over medium heat until the sugar dissolves. Add the rice and stir continuously until the mixture comes to the boil. Cover the pan, then transfer to the oven and bake for 30 minutes or until the rice is tender and has absorbed all the milk. Remove the rice from the oven, uncover, place a tea towel over the top and leave to stand until just warm.

4   Meanwhile, whisk the cream until soft peaks form. Fold in the custard cream, then stir the mixture into the rice pudding. Divide the rice pudding among six 150 ml capacity ramekins and refrigerate for 1 hour or until lightly chilled before serving.

Serves 6

Far Breton
PRUNE CUSTARD FLAN

Far means flour in the Breton dialect and this is a very traditional local dish. It's really more of a tea-time thing than something you'd serve after a big meal as it is quite substantial – it was designed to fill up hungry stomachs after all. I'd serve it in the mid-afternoon with a cup of tea.

125 g unsalted butter, plus extra for greasing
200 g caster sugar
1 litre milk
300 g pitted prunes
50 ml dark rum
6 egg yolks
250 g plain flour

1   Place the butter, 100 g of the sugar and 750 ml of the milk in a saucepan and stir over low heat just until the butter is melted. Remove the pan from the heat, then add the remaining milk and set aside until cool.

2   Meanwhile, place the prunes and rum in a bowl. Add enough boiling water to just cover the prunes, then leave to stand for 20 minutes. (It can help the prunes absorb the liquid if you microwave them on low for a few minutes before soaking.)

3   Preheat the oven to 180°C. Grease a deep 24 cm round cake tin with the extra butter.

4   Place the egg yolks and remaining 100 g sugar in the bowl of an electric mixer and whisk until thick and pale. Gradually sift in the flour and whisk until smooth, then whisk in the milk mixture until a smooth batter forms. Strain through a fine-mesh sieve into a jug.

5   Drain the prunes and pat dry on a tea towel. Scatter the prunes over the base of the prepared tin, then pour the batter over the top. Bake for 40 minutes or until the batter is golden and just set.

6   Serve warm or at room temperature.

Serves 8

Café liégeois
ICED COFFEE

You can serve this as a dessert, rather like the Italian affogato, but it's equally good as a mid-afternoon pick-me-up. I'd stick a straw in it and drink it beside the pool on a hot summer's day!

60 g mascarpone
60 ml pouring cream
15 g icing sugar
1 egg yolk
coffee or vanilla bean ice cream, to serve
60 g speculaas biscuits (see page 209), crushed
80 ml freshly brewed espresso, chilled (optional)
1 quantity Chantilly Cream (see page 207)
cocoa nibs (optional) and speculaas biscuits, to serve

Coffee granita
20 g caster sugar
150 ml freshly-brewed hot espresso
1 tablespoon dark rum

1   To make the coffee granita, combine the sugar and hot espresso in a bowl and stir until the sugar dissolves. Cool, then stir in the rum and place in a shallow container. Freeze the mixture for 3–4 hours, then scrape with a fork to break into small ice crystals and return to the freezer.

2   Meanwhile, place the mascarpone, cream, icing sugar and egg yolk in a bowl and whisk until soft peaks form. Refrigerate until ready to use. (It is best to keep all the ingredients as cold as possible.)

3   Several hours before serving, place 6 tall glasses in the freezer to chill.

4   To serve, place 2 small scoops of ice cream in each chilled glass. Top with a spoonful of the mascarpone cream, a spoonful of granita and a little of the crushed speculaas. Drizzle with some of the cold espresso (if using), then finish with a spoonful of Chantilly cream, a little more granita, some cocoa nibs, if desired, and add a speculaas biscuit.

Serves 6

Bavarois à la framboise
RASPBERRY BAVAROIS

Oh raspberry bavarois! Another of the desserts I first encountered during my apprenticeship. I made a fool of myself the first time I tried making it for my family; it didn't hold together and collapsed in a heap when I served it, but after practising a few times, it quickly became my specialty. When I still lived in France, this was what I always made for family birthdays. I like to serve this with scoops of raspberry sorbet, but this is purely optional.

50 ml water
80 g caster sugar
2½ sheets (5 g) silver strength gelatine (see page 209)
ice cubes
250 g raspberries
150 ml pouring cream
Chantilly Cream (see page 207), raspberry sorbet (optional) and
    mint sprigs, to serve

1   Place the water and sugar in a small saucepan and stir over low heat until the sugar dissolves. Meanwhile, soak the gelatine in iced water for 1–2 minutes or until soft. Remove the gelatine and squeeze out any excess water. Add the gelatine to the hot sugar syrup and stir until dissolved. Add 150 g of the raspberries, then puree the mixture in a blender or food processor until smooth. Set aside to cool.

2   Whisk the pouring cream until soft peaks form; be careful not to over-whip the cream or the bavarois will be grainy. Gently fold the whipped cream into the cooled raspberry mixture until well combined. Divide the raspberry mixture among four 250 ml capacity serving glasses and refrigerate for 4 hours or until set.

3   To serve, place a small spoonful of Chantilly cream on top of each bavarois. Top with the remaining raspberries and a sprig of mint and serve with raspberry sorbet, if desired.

Serves 4

Crêpes suzette
CREPES SUZETTE

This may be THE most famous French restaurant dessert of all. Here I've simplified it for the home cook. However, if you want to show off (like me), you can flambé your crepes in Cointreau in front of your guests (just don't burn your house down!). Originally the crepes were made using Grand Marnier but my uncle was the CEO for Cointreau for years so I'm a bit biased.

2 eggs
30 g caster sugar
360 ml milk
250 g plain flour
80 g unsalted butter
pinch of table salt

Orange sauce
2 large oranges
180 g caster sugar
30 g unsalted butter, chopped
1½ tablespoons Cointreau
1½ tablespoons cognac

1 Whisk the eggs and sugar together in a large bowl and then add the milk. Sift the flour into the egg mixture, whisking continuously until the batter is the consistency of thick cream.

2 Melt the butter in a small saucepan, then add 1 tablespoon to the crepe batter, along with a pinch of salt.

3 Heat a 20 cm non-stick frying pan over medium heat, then add 1 teaspoon of the melted butter to coat the base of the pan. Add a ladleful (about 50 ml) of crepe batter, turning the pan to coat the base completely. Cook the batter for 1 minute or until you see the edges of the crepe beginning to crisp and loosen from the sides and the base of the crepe is light golden. Turn over and cook for another 10–15 seconds. Transfer to a plate and keep warm. Repeat with the remaining melted butter and crepe batter, stacking the crepes on top of each other as you go. (Makes 12 crepes.)

4 To make the orange sauce, use a vegetable peeler to remove the zest of the orange in wide strips, then cut off and discard the bitter white pith using a small, sharp knife. Cut the zest into julienne (see page 209).

5 Place the zest in a small saucepan, cover with cold water and bring to the boil. Drain the zest, then repeat this process twice. Juice the oranges, then strain the orange juice into a jug; you should have 250 ml. Combine the orange zest and 120 g of the sugar in a bowl and rub them together with your fingertips.

6 Sprinkle the remaining sugar into the warm frying pan, then cook over medium heat until the sugar melts and turns golden. Add the orange juice and orange zest mixture and stir to melt the sugar. Add the butter and shake the pan until it is combined with the orange sauce, then remove from the heat. Working one at a time, and using tongs, place a crepe into the orange sauce, fold in half, then half again and spoon over a little sauce. Remove from the pan, allowing the excess sauce to drain back into the pan and transfer to a serving plate. Repeat with the remaining crepes. Add the Cointreau and cognac to the pan, moving the pan off the heat to flambe, if desired.

7 To serve, transfer the crepes to a serving plate, then pour over the sauce.

Serves 6

Clafoutis aux cerises
CHERRY CLAFOUTIS

Purists say you should leave the cherry stones in for added flavour but if you don't want to wreck your dental work, I say take them out. You can infuse the milk up to one day ahead and refrigerate it until needed. Clafoutis is a straightforward dessert to make but its success lies in using fresh cherries, not frozen (or use a drained 680 g jar of pitted sour cherries). And in not overcooking it or the batter will go tough. Oh, and in always serving it warm, never cold.

250 ml milk
½ vanilla pod, seeds scraped
50 g unsalted butter, melted and cooled, plus
    softened butter for greasing
4 eggs
125 g caster sugar
table salt
80 g plain flour
1½ tablespoons Kirsch
500 g ripe pitted cherries
icing sugar, for dusting

1 Place the milk, vanilla seeds and the pod in a small saucepan over low heat and bring to just below a simmer. Remove from the heat and leave to infuse for 1 hour. Strain the milk through a fine-mesh sieve into a jug and discard the vanilla pod.

2 Preheat the oven to 180°C. Grease a 1.5 litre capacity gratin dish with the extra softened butter.

3 Process the eggs, sugar and a pinch of salt in a blender for 1–2 minutes or until smooth. Add the cooled melted butter and the warm milk and combine well. Sift the flour over the top of the egg mixture, then add the Kirsch and blend until smooth and well combined. Strain through a fine-mesh sieve into a jug.

4 Scatter the cherries evenly over the base of the gratin dish, then carefully pour the custard mixture over the top. Bake the clafoutis for 25–30 minutes or until golden and just set.

5 To serve, dust the clafoutis with icing sugar and serve immediately.

Serves 6

Pithiviers
ALMOND TORTE

Also known as *galettes des rois*, this beautiful cake is traditionally served for Epiphany on January 6; in France it is traditional to hide a clay trinket inside. The smallest child then chooses a slice for each person around the table – who ever receives the slice with the trinket gets to wear a crown and be king for the day. It is so easy to put together because you don't need to make your own puff pastry as there are some great ready-made brands available now.

50 g soft unsalted butter
100 g caster sugar
100 g ground almonds
2 eggs
1 tablespoon rum or brandy
a few drops of almond extract
2 sheets ready-rolled butter puff pastry, thawed
1 egg yolk, combined with 1 teaspoon water

1 Using the paddle attachment of an electric mixer, beat the butter and sugar until smooth and creamy. Add the ground almonds and combine well, then add the eggs, rum and almond extract and beat until smooth. Refrigerate for 30 minutes.

2 Cut out a 20 cm round from one sheet of the pastry and place on a baking tray lined with baking paper. Brush the edge with the beaten egg yolk mixture. Spoon the almond mixture over the base, leaving a 3 cm border. Cut a 23 cm round from the other sheet of pastry and place over the top of the filling, pressing gently but firmly to remove any air pockets and to seal the edges well. Use a small sharp knife to cut a small hole in the top of the pastry to allow steam to escape. Brush the top all over with the egg yolk mixture and refrigerate for 30 minutes.

3 Preheat the oven to 180°C.

4 Using a small sharp knife, lightly decorate the top the top of the pastry in a star or spiral pattern, making sure not to cut all the way through. Bake for 30–35 minutes or until the pastry is golden and puffed.

5 Serve warm or at room temperature.

Serves 6

Tarte aux poires bourdaloue
PEAR AND ALMOND TART

This tart takes me back to my time as an apprentice as though it were only yesterday. It also reminds me that a dish doesn't have to be complicated to be truly great. The combination of pear and almonds is simply gorgeous and I'll let you in on a secret: I don't mind if you use tinned pears here. Actually, they are the only tinned fruit that I'll allow you to use!

1 quantity Sweet Shortcrust Pastry (see page 206)
plain flour, for dusting
50 g soft unsalted butter
100 g caster sugar
100 g ground almonds
2 eggs
1 tablespoon rum or brandy
1 teaspoon almond extract
1 × 790 g tin pear halves in syrup, drained and
    patted dry, then halved lengthways
creme fraiche or double cream (optional), to serve

1   Roll out the pastry on a lightly floured work surface until 4 mm thick, then use to line a 25 cm tart tin with a removable base. Use a small sharp knife to trim off excess pastry. Refrigerate for 30 minutes.

2   Preheat the oven to 160°C.

3   Place the butter and sugar in a bowl and, using hand-held electric beaters, beat until light and fluffy. Stir in the ground almonds, then add the eggs, rum and almond extract and beat to combine well. Spoon the almond filling into the tart shell and smooth the top. Place the pear halves, cut-side down, on a chopping board and cut widthways incisions into the pear, at 5 mm intervals, taking care not to cut all the way through. Use a spatula to lift each pear half onto the almond cream, spacing them evenly around the tart (see opposite).

4   Bake the tart for 35–40 minutes or until the pastry and filling are golden. Serve warm or at room temperature with creme fraiche or double cream. Best eaten on day of making.

Serves 6

Soupe de fruits rouges et son sorbet au yaourt

BERRY SOUP WITH YOGHURT SORBET

I call this dish 'summer in a bowl', especially as you must use fresh berries when they are in season – frozen ones just don't have the same lively taste. Red wine gives the berries a lovely little lift and the tangy yoghurt sorbet is delicious and so easy to make. Children love this as much as adults, even though it's a little bit on the sophisticated side.

100 g strawberries, hulled and halved or quartered
100 g raspberries
100 g blackberries
100 g blueberries
200 ml light red wine (such as pinot noir)
50 g caster sugar
1 vanilla pod, seeds scraped
extra mixed berries, to serve

Yoghurt sorbet
150 g caster sugar
150 g liquid glucose (see page 209)
300 ml water
750 g thick natural Greek-style yoghurt

1 To make the yoghurt sorbet, place the sugar, glucose and water in a small saucepan and bring to the boil over medium heat, stirring often until the sugar dissolves and the mixture is smooth. Remove from the heat and leave to stand until cool, then refrigerate until cold.

2 Place the yoghurt in a large bowl, whisk in the cooled syrup, then churn the mixture in an ice-cream machine according to the manufacturer's instructions. (Makes about 1 litre. Sorbet will keep in the freezer for 6 weeks.)

3 Place half of the berries in a large bowl and, using the back of a large spoon, crush well. Add the remaining whole berries, wine, sugar and vanilla seeds and stir to combine well. Leave to stand for 2 hours, stirring occasionally. Blend the mixture in a blender to form a smooth puree.

4 To serve, ladle the berry soup into shallow bowls, then place a quenelle (egg-shaped spoonful, see page 209) of sorbet in the middle and surround with extra berries.

Serves 4

Pâte brisée
SHORTCRUST PASTRY

250 g plain flour
large pinch fine sea salt
1 egg yolk
125 g unsalted butter, chopped and softened
    to room temperature
50 ml cold water

Sift the flour and salt into a large bowl and make a well in the centre. Add the egg yolk, butter and water and use your fingertips to work them into the dry ingredients until a dough forms; it doesn't have to be perfect.

Turn the dough out onto a lightly floured surface and knead gently and quickly using the palm of your hand until just combined. (It is better for the dough to be a little rough rather than to overwork it, and you must work quickly to prevent the butter from melting.) Shape the dough into a disc, wrap in plastic film and refrigerate for 1 hour before using.

Makes enough to line a 30 cm tart tin

Pâte sablée
SWEET SHORTCRUST PASTRY

125 g unsalted butter, chopped and softened
    to room temperature
1 egg
90 g icing sugar, sifted
30 g ground almonds
250 g plain flour, sifted

Place the butter, egg, icing sugar and ground almonds in the bowl of an electric mixer and beat with a paddle attachment until smooth and well combined.

Add the flour a little at a time and, as soon as all the flour is just incorporated, stop mixing. Transfer the dough to a bench-top and shape into a disc, then wrap in plastic film and refrigerate overnight. Remove from the refrigerator 30 minutes before using.

Makes enough to line a 30 cm tart tin

Pâte sablée au chocolat
CHOCOLATE SHORTCRUST PASTRY

150 g plain flour
100 g Dutch-process cocoa (see page 208)
125 g unsalted butter, at room temperature, chopped
1 egg
90 g icing sugar, sifted
30 g ground almonds

Sift the flour and cocoa into a bowl and stir to combine.

Using an electric mixer fitted with a paddle attachment (or a wooden spoon) beat the butter, egg, icing sugar and ground almonds until smooth. Gradually add the flour and cocoa mixture; stop beating as soon as the mixture comes together to form a dough. Do not overwork the dough or the pastry will be tough.

Shape the dough into a disc, cover with plastic film and refrigerate for at least 12 hours before using.

Makes enough to line a 30 cm tart tin

Crème Chantilly
CHANTILLY CREAM

100 ml pouring cream
½ vanilla pod, seeds scraped
20 g caster sugar

Place the cream and vanilla seeds in a bowl and stir in the sugar. Whisk the cream until soft peaks form. (Be careful not to over-whip the cream or you will make butter!)

Makes about 175 ml

Crème Anglaise
CUSTARD CREAM

500 ml milk
1 vanilla pod, seeds scraped
ice cubes
6 egg yolks
125 g caster sugar

Place the milk, vanilla seeds and the pod in a heavy-based saucepan over medium heat. Bring to just below the boil, then remove from the heat and leave to stand for 30 minutes to infuse.

Place a fine-mesh sieve over a bowl, then place that bowl in another larger bowl of iced water and set aside.

Place the egg yolks and sugar in a large bowl and use a whisk until thick and pale. Whisking continuously, gradually add the warm milk, then return the mixture to the pan and stir over low heat for 10 minutes or until it thickens enough to coat the back of a wooden spoon. The custard should reach 80°C on a candy thermometer (see page 208) and not above or it will scramble. Immediately pour the custard into the sieve sitting over the bowl placed over the iced water and whisk for 1–2 minutes to allow the heat to escape.

Leave the custard to stand until cool, whisking occasionally. (The custard will keep in an airtight container in the refrigerator for up to 7 days.)

Makes 650 ml

GLOSSARY

Anchovy fillets – salted
Made from anchovies, still in their skins, soaked in oil or brine and often sold in tins.

Back-fat – pork
A cut of pork which comes from the pig's back. It can be wrapped around other meats and also used in terrines and pates. You will need to order this in advance from a good-quality butcher.

Batons
Vegetable sticks cut to a uniform size.

Blowtorch – kitchen
Used in the kitchen for a number of purposes, most commonly for desserts such as creme brulee.

Bouquet garni
A bundle of herbs (usually parsley, thyme and a bay leaf and sometimes including lemon or orange rind) tied together with kitchen string and used in soups, braises or a stockpot to add flavour. My standard bouquet garni consists of two thyme sprigs and a fresh bay leaf, wrapped in a piece of the green part of a leek, then tied with string.

Candy/deep-fry thermometer
Used when making jams and sugar syrup-based sweets to measure the different stages of sugar syrup leading to caramel. Also use to measure oil temperature for deep-frying.

Cartouche
A round of baking paper placed directly over a liquid dish such as a braise, casserole, stew or custard to prevent a skin from forming on the surface. It also helps to keep the ingredients moist by preventing the liquid from evaporating.

Caul fat (crépinette)
The thin, fatty, lacy, web-like membrane surrounding the internal organs of animals such as cows, sheep and pigs. It adds flavour and a protective coating to meat, including pate mixtures, during cooking. Available from good-quality butchers; you may need to order in advance.

Chocolate – couverture
Top-quality chocolate with a high level of cocoa butter. To be classified as couverture, a chocolate must contain a minimum of thirty-two per cent cocoa butter and fifty-four per cent combined total of cocoa solids and cocoa butter. Available from specialty food stores.

Clarified butter – making
To clarify butter, melt the butter in a small saucepan over low heat, then simmer until the milk solids separate and fall to the bottom, being careful not to burn the butter. Strain off the clear butter and discard the milk solids. The remaining liquid is clarified butter.

Cocoa powder – Dutch-process
Cocoa is the powder remaining after the cocoa butter has been removed from the bean. Dutch-processed cocoa powder is unsweetened cocoa treated with an alkali to neutralise its acids.

Cornichons
Small pickled cucumbers. Available from delicatessens and specialty food stores.

Crab – preparation
Hold the blue swimmer crab upside-down, lift the tail flaps (or 'apron') and insert a small knife under the top shell. Twist the knife to loosen and pull off the top shell, then remove and discard the grey gills ('dead man's fingers'). Leave the coral (mustard) as it holds a lot of flavour. Using a kitchen cleaver or large sharp knife, cut each crab body into 8 pieces, then proceed with the recipe.

Dijon mustard – French
Mustard made with brown or black mustard seeds, with various herbs, according to traditional methods. Wholegrain Dijon mustard is made by mixing whole mustard seeds with white wine and spices. I use the French brand, Maille, available from most supermarkets.

Espelette pepper
Deep red chilli pepper produced in the Basque region of France and named after the town of Espelette. Available from specialty food stores.

Fleur de sel
A natural sea salt, rich in minerals, harvested by hand in Brittany, France. Available from specialty food stores.

French-trimming – meat

French trimming is a decorative way of presenting a piece of meat, stripped of all fat and skin, with a piece of bone protruding. Used for cutlets including lamb, pork and veal, as well as shanks.

Gelatine – leaf

Gelatine is a gelling agent derived from collagen used to set jellies, mousses and sweets. It comes in powder or leaf form and the leaves come in different grades: titanium, gold and silver, according to how easily they set. Titanium-strength leaves are the strongest and silver are the weakest, with gold somewhere in the middle. Gelatine leaves must be soaked in hot water prior to use. Available from specialty food stores and good-quality delicatessens.

Glucose – liquid

A 'single' sugar in the form of syrup commonly used in commercial kitchens instead of sugar to make ice cream, sorbet and confectionery. It often replaces a proportion of white sugar in recipes. Available from health food stores.

Julienne

A technique for cutting vegetables into matchstick-size strips of uniform length.

Lardons

Small pieces of pork fat, bacon, speck or pancetta that are sauteed. Used as a salad garnish or inserted into large pieces of meat to keep them moist during cooking.

Lemon – segmenting

To segment a lemon, remove the skin and pith, then cut the flesh into segments, discarding the frame.

Mushrooms – morel

Regarded as a delicacy, morels are hollow and have a honeycomb-like surface which traps dirt. Generally brown in colour, though some are black, they should be cooked before eating. Available from good-quality food stores.

Nuts – toasting flaked almonds and pine nuts

The best way to toast pine nuts and flaked almonds is to roast them on a baking tray in the oven at 180°C for 3–4 minutes or until golden.

Quatre épices

A combination of four spices, usually pepper, ginger, nutmeg and cloves, used to flavour casseroles, sausages and terrines. You can make it yourself or buy it from specialty food stores.

Quenelle

Traditionally made from minced fish or meat, bound with seasoning and egg, that is formed into an oval and poached in stock or water. Today the term describes the process of shaping soft foods such as ice cream, vegetable puree or chocolate mousse between two spoons to form a three-sided egg-like shape.

Snails – tinned

The most widely used snails in cooking are the petit gris, the common or garden snail, and the larger vineyard or burgundy snail. Tinned ones are ready to eat and are available from specialty food stores.

Speck

This spiced, salt-cured, smoked pork product is used to flavour soups and casseroles or cut into lardons and used to garnish salads.

Speculaas

These thin, very crunchy, slightly browned biscuits have an image or figure (often from traditional stories about Saint Nicholas) stamped on the front before baking; the back is flat. Often sold labelled as Dutch Windmill biscuits in Australia, New Zealand and the United States.

Tomatoes – peeling

Make a cross at one end and remove the core at the other end. Dunk the tomatoes in boiling water for 30 seconds, then immediately transfer to iced water. Drain, then peel off their skins and squeeze out the seeds.

Vermouth

A fortified white wine, flavoured with herbs and spices, used as an aperitif.

Vinegar – sherry

Made in Spain from sherry and aged in oak for at least six months. Used in salad dressings and for deglazing. Available from specialty food stores.

MERCI

Writing this book has been a long-held dream of mine and now that I've finally accomplished it there are a few people who have been there in one way or another along the journey that I need to thank.

Firstly, thank you to the team at Penguin: my publisher, Julie Gibbs, for her belief in and vision for my book; managing editor Ingrid Ohlsson, who has been a great support and help; Kathleen Gandy for her editing and Kirby Armstrong for the wonderful design. Thanks also to Leanne Kitchen for putting my words into order and telling my story and to Christine Osmond for testing the recipes. Thanks too to Nicole Abadee and Arielle Gamble.

Huge thanks to the wonderful team that helped me get the pictures on to the page – 'The Manuettes'! Chris Chen, your photographs are amazing. Thanks to Geraldine Muñoz for the styling and giving my book the look I wanted and to Megan Pigott for her creative eye and love of everything chocolate!

To Alban Badet, thanks for all your help in writing the recipes and preparing them for the photography – I couldn't have done it without you, buddy!

To Natalie Street, who arrived at the right time in my hectic life, what can I say? Natalie is the person that every busy individual wishes for; I couldn't do any of this without her and she has now also become a great friend.

Thanks also to my agent, Justine May, who discovered my talent and believed and continues to believe in me.

Thanks to Yannick Besnard and Michele Guai, my business partners at L'étoile, for all your understanding and support. To my terrific Head Chef, Troy, plus the entire team at L'étoile: thank you for keeping the restaurant running when I am unable to be around.

To my close friends here and all over the world, thanks for always being there and giving me support, and a drink, when I need it!

To Ronnie, thanks for dealing with my highs and lows throughout my career; I wouldn't be where I am today without your support.

I also wish to thank the following people and businesses for generously supplying props for the photographs: Sally Beresford, Bisanna Tiles, Bison Home, Bridget Bodenham, Dinosaur Designs, Malcolm Greenwood, Ici et La, Mud Australia, Perfect Pieces and Peter's of Kensington.

And finally to my family (*et enfin ma famille*): *Maman, merci pour ton support éternelle et pour mon éducation – surtout culinaire, c'est pour cela que ce livre est remplit de souvenir d'enfance.* (Mum, you have always been supportive of me and my goals, thank you for the inspiration you have given me for many of the recipes in this book.)

Merci à mon père, qui m'a donné mon premier travail et qui m'a fait découvrir toutes les facettes de la restauration. (To my father, thank you for kick-starting my interest in the restaurant industry and giving me my first job in a kitchen!)

And last, but by no means least, to my son Jonti – you are the reason I do all of this. You give me energy and inspiration every day. I LOVE YOU!

INDEX

LANTERN

Published by the Penguin Group
Penguin Group (Australia)
250 Camberwell Road, Camberwell, Victoria 3124, Australia
(a division of Pearson Australia Group Pty Ltd)
Penguin Group (USA) Inc.
375 Hudson Street, New York, New York 10014, USA
Penguin Group (Canada)
10 Alcorn Avenue, Toronto, Ontario, Canada M4V 3B2
(a division of Pearson Penguin Canada Inc.)
Penguin Books Ltd
80 Strand, London WC2R 0RL, England
Penguin Ireland
25 St Stephen's Green, Dublin 2, Ireland
(a division of Penguin Books Ltd)
Penguin Books India Pvt Ltd
11 Community Centre, Panchsheel Park, New Delhi – 110 017, India
Penguin Group (NZ)
Cnr Airborne and Rosedale Roads, Albany, Auckland, New Zealand
(a division of Pearson New Zealand Ltd)
Penguin Books (South Africa) (Pty) Ltd
24 Sturdee Avenue, Rosebank, Johannesburg 2196, South Africa

Penguin Books Ltd, Registered Offices: 80 Strand, London,
WC2R 0RL, England

First published by Penguin Group (Australia), a division of
Pearson Australia Group Pty Ltd, 2011

10 9 8 7 6 5 4 3 2 1

Design by Kirby Armstrong © Penguin Group (Australia)
Styling by Geraldine Muñoz
Typeset in Franklin Gothic 9/11.5 by Post Pre-press Group,
Carina Heights, Queensland
Colour reproduction by Splitting Image Colour Studio Pty Ltd,
Clayton, Victoria
Printed and bound in China by 1010 Printing International Limited

National Library of Australia
Cataloguing-in-Publication data:

Feildel, Manu, 1973 –

1st ed.

ISBN 9781921382505 (hbk.)

Includes index.

French cuisine, Cookery.

641.5944

penguin.com.au